YORK NOTES

…ou Like It

William Shakespeare

Notes by Robin Sowerby

 Longman  York Press

YORK PRESS
322 Old Brompton Road, London SW5 9JH

PEARSON EDUCATION LIMITED
Edinburgh Gate, Harlow,
Essex CM20 2JE, United Kingdom
Associated companies, branches and representatives throughout the world

First published 1999
Second impression 2001

ISBN 0-582-41461-X

Designed by Vicki Pacey, Trojan Horse, London
Phototypeset by Gem Graphics, Trenance, Mawgan Porth, Cornwall
Colour reproduction and film output by Spectrum Colour
Produced by Pearson Education North Asia Limited, Hong Kong

Contents

Part four

Textual analysis

Part five

Background

Part six

Critical history and broader perspectives

PART ONE

INTRODUCTION

HOW TO STUDY A PLAY

Studying on your own requires self-discipline and a carefully thought-out work plan in order to be effective.

- Drama is a special kind of writing (the technical term is **genre**) because it needs a performance in the theatre to arrive at a full interpretation of its meaning. Try to imagine that you are a member of the audience when reading the play. Think about how it could be presented on the stage, not just about the words on the page.
- Drama is always about conflict of some sort (which may be below the surface). Identify the conflicts in the play and you will be close to identifying the large ideas or themes which bind all the parts together.
- Make careful notes on themes, character, plot and any sub-plots of the play.
- Why do you like or dislike the characters in the play? How do your feelings towards them develop and change?
- Playwrights find non-realistic ways of allowing an audience to see into the minds and motives of their characters, for example soliloquy, aside or music. Consider how such dramatic devices are used in the play you are studying.
- Think of the playwright writing the play. Why were these particular arrangements of events, characters and speeches chosen?
- Cite exact sources for all quotations, whether from the text itself or from critical commentaries. Wherever possible find your own examples from the play to back up your opinions.
- Always express your ideas in your own words.

This York Note offers an introduction to *As You Like It* and cannot substitute for close reading of the text and the study of secondary sources.

In the Shakespeare canon, *As You Like It* occupies a secure place as one of his most successful comedies, a play written in his artistic maturity that together with *Twelfth Night* (1599) represents the peak of his comic achievement. The underlying simple general formula of this romantic comedy – boy meets girl, they fall in love and after a variety of obstacles and misunderstandings have been overcome, they marry to live happily ever after – is an archetype that has always pleased audiences. To evoke the archetype, however, is to see immediately that much of the attraction of *As You Like It* stems from the fact that the play is an unusual variation on this well-tried and familiar formula. Principally, it is not so much an instance of boy meeting girl but of girl meeting boy, for the female lead, Rosalind, indeed takes the lead in doing all the wooing, so that the play provides a representation of the **romance** theme that is unconventional in any literature before the twentieth century. And it is, of course, the female lead upon whom all the dramatic and critical attention is focused: the heroine Rosalind is the star part in the play and has claims to be Shakespeare's strongest and most attractive female character (certainly stronger than Viola in *Twelfth Night*) whose only rival might be Cleopatra, from his later Roman play *Antony and Cleopatra* (1606–7). Though played by a boy on the Elizabethan stage, Rosalind for women like Hamlet for men is the classic acting part that has inaugurated many a successful career. Among acclaimed stage Rosalinds have been those of Edith Evans, Peggy Ashcroft, Katherine Hepburn, Vanessa Redgrave and Helen Mirren.

As a character, Rosalind is attractive not because, like Hamlet, we see into her mind through a series of poetic **soliloquies**, but because she has in abundance another characteristic that she does share with Hamlet, a fine verbal inventiveness and **wit**. In his tragic situation Hamlet's wit proves to be somewhat mordant, notably in the graveyard scene, but in this comedy Rosalind's exuberant wit is the expression of an essentially happy nature falling in love and its effect is exhilarating and liberating. It is a characteristic she shares with other members of the cast, notably the two companions who accompany her into the forest, her cousin Celia and Touchstone, the professional jester. Other characters can also be witty; there is verbal ingenuity and **wordplay** in scenes featuring the melancholy Jaques and even Orlando, the male lead, can engage successfully in repartee. The play, as befits a comedy, abounds in verbal jokes and witty argument of which Rosalind proves to be if not the chief exponent (perhaps Touchstone vies with her here) then certainly the most sympathetic.

Rosalind's is such an attractive part because, like Hamlet feigning madness, she has to act herself within the play when she goes into the Forest of Arden disguised as a page boy Ganymede. In Shakespeare's plot, she then takes the lead and dominates the action, until, unlike Hamlet, through her own ingenuity she successfully orchestrates a triumphant **denouement**. The device of disguise, deployed particularly but not only in comedy, is as old as literature itself; there is a famous example of it in the oldest western poem, the *Odyssey* of Homer, when Odysseus disguises himself as a beggar on his return home in order to discover for himself exactly what has been going on in his house during his long absence. But it can be claimed that the use of disguise in *As You Like It* is one of the most successful and entertaining deployments of this conventional technique in the whole of literature.

In the plot the disguise is well motivated for practical reasons, but Rosalind uses it to woo her lover Orlando, unbeknown to him, to test him and perhaps to educate him. The resulting **dramatic irony** that arises when the dramatist creates and exploits a discrepancy between what the characters know and what the audience knows is highly comic and entertaining. Rosalind is able to expose the shallowness and absurdity of conventional modes of wooing. Additionally it can be said that cross-dressing is inherently intriguing and invariably comic. We only have to think of the fascination of pantomime or of the most tawdry cabaret acts. What adds to the fascination and intrigue in the sophisticated work of art that constitutes *As You Like It* is the fact that the success of the disguise prompts serious thought about the great divide between the sexes that involves us all and makes us wonder too about the extent to which our behaviour as women and men is innate and biologically determined or learned and assumed.

Although it may properly be called a romantic comedy, *As You Like It* is not the kind of romantic comedy that might be found currently showing in London's West End or New York's Broadway. In its opening act, we are told about a usurpation and witness the consequences of it, we see a brother maliciously plotting his brother's death and then witness the unjust banishment of the play's heroine. The play starts with a serious presentation of the propensity of human beings to evil and so with the potential for tragedy. Although it cannot really be called a **tragicomedy** since evil is turned to good and a happy outcome is the resolution for all, the play is more of a mixed kind than is generally the case in comedy. This mixture allows us to feel that the dramatist has more than one perspective upon human life and that his drama, wherever it leads, starts from the realities of life as we experience them.

All the way through the play the comic and the serious are mixed in a variety of ways and it is one of the rare excellencies of the play that it has this variety throughout in mood and tone. The two characters who most obviously reflect the opposite poles of this variety are Touchstone the clown who is purely comic and the melancholy Jaques who is a variation of a character more familiar in Elizabethan tragedy, the alienated **malcontent**. Jaques utters what is the most famous speech in the play and indeed one of the most well-known set pieces in the whole of Shakespeare on the seven ages of man 'All the world's a stage, / And all the men and women merely players' (II.7.140ff). The speech is a melancholy utterance of a kind not obviously associated with comedy.

The play's variety is reflected in its linguistic texture. There are grand poetic speeches like that of Jaques or the speech in which the exiled Duke praises the quality of life in the Forest of Arden (II.1.1ff). There are poetic set pieces of a different kind when the characters express their feelings of love (for example, the lyrical litany involving Rosalind, Orlando, Silvius, and Phebe beginning at V.2.78). There is a very different and simpler kind of poetic beauty in the various songs, including the much anthologised 'Under the greenwood tree', (II.5.1), 'Blow, blow, thou winter wind' (II.7.175) and 'It was a lover and his lass' (V.3.15). By contrast, much of the play is written in a fast-moving, elegant and witty prose that sparkles with repartee.

Another aspect of the play's variety is reflected in the setting and the contrast that is felt throughout between life at court and life in the country in the Forest of Arden. The contrast here represents one of the play's basic themes. The evocation of a retired life in the natural world of the Forest of Arden, 'under the greenwood tree' away from what the exiled Duke calls the 'painted pomp' of 'the envious court' (II.1.3–4), has always been felt to be one of the play's greatest attractions. The Forest of

Arden is one of Shakespeare's most celebrated settings and has given its name to a prestigious and long-standing edition of his plays: the Arden Shakespeare. It is not that there is any great set piece description of the forest itself; in fact, there is remarkably little in the way of direct physical or poetic description. Rather the forest represents an alternative world, not wholly idealised for its natives have to endure the harshness of winter and wind, but one in which human beings live a simpler and more natural life away from the competitive rat race of life in the city where behaviour is often far from civilised. Arden therefore is an idea in the mind evoking a nostalgia for a simpler past and a desire for a simpler present that most people readily fall into and embrace at least for the duration of the play. This nostalgia and wishful thinking is gently mocked when at the end the exiles who have made the best of their lot in the forest and vowed never to return to the court do so immediately and without hesitation as soon as the opportunity is offered to them.

Unlike the Athenian wood into which the courtiers disappear in Shakespeare's earlier romantic comedy *A Midsummer Night's Dream* (1595), the forest is not a fantastic place inhabited by elves and fairies, the stuff of which dreams are made, nor is it like the enchanted island in Shakespeare's late **romance** *The Tempest* (1611) on which the exiled Duke Prospero is shipwrecked and exerts control through magic by virtue of his mastery of the world of spirits. There is, comparatively speaking, a pervading realism in *As You Like It*, yet strange things do happen in the forest even if they do so without obvious supernatural aid. The wicked Oliver has a close encounter with a snake and a lioness before he is saved by the good nature of his brother Orlando whereupon he undergoes a miraculous amendment of life and suddenly becomes eligible for reciprocal love at first sight with Celia. The wicked Duke, arriving at the edge of the forest with an army to capture and kill the exiles, is subject to a sudden spiritual conversion after an encounter with a hermit. The forest not only represents an alternative world to life at court but it is a world where human wickedness does not and perhaps cannot prosper. It has a benignly transforming effect that makes it, figuratively speaking, a magical place and an imaginative world that we all might wish into existence as an alternative to the banal common-sense everyday reality, where the wicked prosper and happy endings are not so common, that we know only too well.

Not everybody has been susceptible to the magic as Shakespeare has contrived it in the resolution of his plot. Indeed criticism of the plot is the most common of adverse reactions to *As You Like It*. In the first place, it has often been said that after the first act, when the scene shifts to the forest, not much happens in the play. Unfavourable comparisons have been made with the more dynamic and intriguing plot of *Twelfth Night*. The sudden conversions of the wicked characters have been felt to be unsatisfactory. Samuel Johnson (1709–84), for example, lamented that we are not privy to the dialogue between the wicked Duke and hermit and felt that Shakespeare had missed an opportunity for our moral improvement here. The suddenness with which Celia and Oliver fall in love and come to the point of marriage has also been felt to be unsatisfactory. This latter may be said to be a comic comment on the protracted nature of courtly love; the sensible Celia's sudden fall may also be regarded as a further illustration of the theme that love is a kind of folly if not madness itself. But such defences may not convince sceptics. There is perhaps a genuine difficulty here arising from a potential conflict between the conventions and demands of a fanciful romance on the one hand and the habitual psychological realism with which Shakespeare invests character and motive on the other. Does Shakespeare always succeed in achieving a convincing blend between the two?

In the twentieth century there is a further question about the ending. In much of the action prior to the marriages at the end, through the deployment of Rosalind's disguise there has been a subversion of the usual subordination of women to fathers and husbands. All this is reversed at the end with the restoration of the status quo. Or is it?

Part two

Summaries & commentaries

On internal grounds and from contemporary documentary sources *As You Like It* is usually thought to have been written between 1598 and 1600. The earliest text of the play is to be found in the First Folio, an edition of thirty-six plays by Shakespeare. These were collected together by two fellow actor-sharers in the King's Company, John Heminges and Henry Condell in 1623, some years after Shakespeare's death. Many of the other plays were also published in Quarto editions soon after performance in Shakespeare's lifetime. There is no Quarto edition of *As You Like It*. Uniquely among Shakespeare's plays the folio text has divisions into acts and scenes. Textual scholars report that the folio text, from which all subsequent editions are derived, is a good one, presenting fewer problems than some other Shakespeare plays.

References in this book are to *As You Like It* in The New Penguin Shakespeare edited by H.J. Oliver (Penguin, 1968, and reprinted many times; reprinted with a revised Further Reading in 1996). Readers who are using another edition will find that often the line numbers do not quite agree. And in some cases the discrepancies can be as much as ten or so lines. This is not because one text has more or fewer actual lines than another, but because they are counted differently. Any scene containing prose, and much of this play is in prose, will be numbered to accord with the printing of the prose which will vary from edition to edition and in the case of verse practice will vary in the counting of half lines. Where a speaker ends in mid-line and another speaker seems to complete the half line, if the number of syllables or feet exceed that in a regular iambic pentameter, the two halves will be given a separate line number by some editors. Spelling and punctuation will differ from edition to edition depending upon editorial policy concerning modernisation.

Different editions offer different kinds of help to the reader. Most modern editions are prepared with notes. In the case of The Arden, edited by Agnes Latham (Methuen, 1975, Thomas Nelson, 1997) and The Oxford Shakespeare, edited by Alan Brissenden (The World's

Classics, Oxford, 1993), these are extensive and helpfully located below the text. The Signet Shakespeare, edited by Alan Gilman (The New American Library, New York, 1963) reprints generous excerpts form Shakespeare's main source for the play – the prose **romance** *Rosalynde* by Thomas Lodge, referred to and discussed here in Critical Approaches. Both the Arden and Oxford editions have extensive accounts of the stage history of the play. A particular feature of the Oxford edition is the identification of bawdy double meanings in the commentary on the text where details of the stage history are also given suggesting often that reading and performance of the play prior to the twentieth century was significantly more sentimentalised.

SYNOPSIS

Act I is set in the court of Duke Frederick who has ousted his elder brother Duke Senior from power and sent him into exile. In the garden of the late Sir Rowland de Boys, his youngest son Orlando complains to his aged servant Adam that Oliver, his elder brother, has not used the thousand crowns set aside by Sir Rowland to bring him up in a manner befitting a gentleman but treats him no better than a servant. Oliver enters and the brothers quarrel. Oliver, who hates his brother, refuses to give Orlando the thousand crowns. He summons the wrestler Charles whose challenge Orlando intends to answer and tricks him into thinking that Orlando will plot against his life if he loses the wrestling match. Charles departs with the intention of disabling him.

Celia, the daughter of Duke Frederick, comforts her cousin Rosalind, daughter of the exiled Duke who had been allowed to remain at court because of her great friendship with Celia. They witness the wrestling match in which Orlando defeats Charles. When the Duke learns that the unknown challenger is the son of Sir Rowland, a former enemy, he brusquely departs; the two cousins compliment him on his success, Rosalind in particular as Sir Rowland had been a friend of her father. Orlando immediately falls in love with Rosalind. Rosalind tells Celia she has fallen in love with Orlando. The Duke enters and banishes Rosalind for alleged disloyalty but actually on the grounds of her popularity. Celia, who has pleaded against her father's decision in vain, determines to accompany her cousin in exile, suggesting that they disguise themselves in humble clothes. Rosalind has the idea of dressing up as a man. Together they determine to depart to seek her father in the Forest of Arden, taking with them the court jester Touchstone for comfort and support.

The opening of Act II and most of the rest of the play is set in the Forest of Arden. In conversation with his lords, the exiled Duke Senior extols the virtues of their life away from the court in the forest. They discuss the attitudes of the melancholy Jaques and the Duke sets out to find him. Back at court, Duke Frederick having discovered their absence, sends for Oliver to help him find Celia and Rosalind whom he believes to be in the company of Orlando. Adam warns Orlando of a plot against his life by Oliver and together they leave his house.

In the Forest, Rosalind disguised as Ganymede and Celia disguised as Aliena overhear the young shepherd Silvius talking to the aged Corin of his love for Phebe. Celia bids Touchstone solicit food from Corin. He says that they can offer little as they work for a mean master who is about to sell their flocks and livelihoods. The women make arrangements for Corin to buy his master's pasture and flock and cottage where they propose to live. The Duke's musician Amiens sings a song 'Under the greenwood tree' in the company of Jaques then goes off to find the Duke as a meal has been prepared for him. In another part of the forest, Orlando comforts the weary Adam and promises to bring him food. As the Duke is about to eat, Jaques rushes in to tell of his meeting with a fool in the forest (Touchstone). Orlando enters abruptly demanding food. The Duke treats him gently; Orlando apologises, pleading necessity. Jaques delivers his great speech 'All the world's a stage'. Amiens sings a song 'Blow, blow, thou winter wind'. The Duke is pleased to discover the identity of Orlando whom he welcomes to his 'court'.

In Act III the courtship begins in earnest. At the opening Duke Frederick charges Oliver with the task of bringing back Orlando dead or alive within a year. In the forest Orlando pins up verses in praise of Rosalind on the trees. Touchstone and Corin debate the merits of life at court and life in the country. Rosalind finds and reads one of Orlando's poems. Touchstone mocks and parodies it. Celia reads another and discloses that Orlando whom she has seen swooning beneath a tree is the author. The women then overhear Orlando get the better of Jaques in a battle of wits. The disguised Rosalind decides to accost Orlando and speak to him 'like a saucy lackey'. She persuades him that she has a cure for love; he is to woo her as if she were his 'Rosalind' and she will behave with all manner of fickleness and so bring him to his senses. Orlando agrees.

There is courtship of a more earthy kind when Touchstone talks to the goat-herd Audrey whom he has decided to marry. Jaques persuades him to marry in church. Rosalind, upset that Orlando has not turned up for their meeting, discusses him with Celia. Corin offers to show them true love (Silvius) being rejected by proud disdain (Phebe). Phebe pitilessly scorns the courtship of Silvius. Rosalind who has observed this intervenes to rebuke her. Phebe immediately falls in love with the disguised Rosalind who rejects her and rebukes her in return. Phebe melts a little in her attitude to Silvius and sees that she can use him to her advantage by getting him to deliver a letter to Rosalind.

Act IV begins with Rosalind getting the better of Jaques in a debate about melancholia. In exuberant form she then chides Orlando for being late, bids him woo her and elicits the aid of Celia in going through a mock marriage with him. When Orlando says he must be away for two hours because he has said that he will dine with the Duke, she warns him not to be a minute late for their next rendezvous or she will think him untrustworthy. After he has departed, Celia rebukes her for going beyond the bounds of their sex in her love-talk. There follows an interlude in which Jaques elicits a song from a forester who has killed a deer that they propose to present to the Duke. Rosalind receives from the hands of Silvius a love letter from Phebe; at first she pretends that it is abusive and that she believes Silvius to be the author. She then reads it to Silvius and rebukes him for his folly in love. Oliver enters in search of Ganymede to deliver a message from Orlando to explain his inability to keep his appointment. He tells how Oliver rescued him from first a snake and then a lion being wounded in the process. Rosalind faints.

Act V begins with Touchstone's threatening dismissal of one of Audrey's previous suitors, William, the country clown. In conversation between the two brothers it emerges that Oliver and Aliena (Celia) have fallen in love at first sight and propose to get married on the following day. When Orlando remarks that it is a bitter thing to look into happiness through another man's eyes, Rosalind promises that she will bring about his own marriage to his Rosalind at the same time. Phebe rebukes Rosalind for revealing the contents of her letter. Silvius defines what it is to be a true lover referring to his own feelings for Phebe; Orlando and Phebe echo his feelings in a refrain as they yearn for Ganymede and Rosalind, while Rosalind joins in with her feeling 'for no woman'. Touchstone announces that he and Audrey will be married the next day, thus confirming the fourth marriage in the play. Two pages sing 'It was a lover and his lass'.

In the final scene, Rosalind, still in disguise, confirms the marriage pacts that she has made in the presence of the Duke. Touchstone arrives with Audrey and engages in a final bout of **wit** as he is introduced to the Duke. Rosalind and Celia then enter out of disguise and Rosalind seals the bargains made. A **masquer** Hymen sings a wedding song. The Duke welcomes his daughter and niece. Phebe accepts Silvius.

Jaques de Boys, the second son of Sir Rowland, comes with the news that Duke Frederick, who had come to the forest with a large army with the intention of capturing Duke Senior and putting him to the sword, had experienced a change of heart on meeting and talking with a religious man at the edge of the forest. He has decided to bequeath his crown to the banished Duke and restore the lands seized from those he banished and to withdraw from the world. There is general rejoicing. So impressed is Jaques with the Duke's conversion that he proposes to follow him into the religious life. It is left to Rosalind to appeal to the audience's goodwill in the epilogue.

ACT I

SCENE 1 Orlando confronts his elder brother Oliver over neglect of his upbringing. Oliver plots against him with the wrestler Charles

In the orchard (garden) of the late Sir Rowland de Boys, his youngest son, Orlando complains to Adam, an old servant, that his older brother Oliver is neglecting to fulfil their father's wishes in failing to provide him with an upbringing fit for a gentleman. Oliver has not spent the thousand crowns set aside by Sir Rowland for the purpose on Orlando's education but treats his brother no better than a servant.

Orlando confronts Oliver with these accusations when he enters. When Oliver angrily threatens his brother, Orlando seizes him by the throat and demands that Oliver either allow him the means to take up gentlemanly pursuits or give him his father's meagre allowance so that he can seek his fortune elsewhere. After Orlando and Adam depart, Oliver, alone on stage, expresses his contempt for his brother and vows that he will not part with the thousand crowns. He then summons Charles, Duke Frederick's wrestler, from whom we learn of the situation at court. The old Duke, Duke Senior, has been ousted from power and banished by his younger brother Duke Frederick. He is living in the Forest of Arden with a number of lords who have joined him and whose lands have been seized by Duke Frederick. Duke Senior's daughter Rosalind has been allowed to stay at court because of her great friendship with Celia, daughter of Duke Frederick.

Charles tells Oliver that he has heard that Orlando wishes to come in disguise to answer his challenge to wrestle with him before the Duke the following day. Fearful for the safety of the young man and conscious of the disgrace that defeat will bring him, he asks Oliver to dissuade him. Oliver replies that he has already attempted this unsuccessfully but Orlando is stubborn, ambitious, envious and forever plotting against his brother. He tells him to use his own judgement but in the same breath hints that he would like him to break his neck; he further warns that if disgraced in the wrestling Orlando will plot against Charles's life. Charles believes Oliver, is grateful for the warning and vows to disable Orlando.

In a **soliloquy**, Oliver reveals his true feelings; he has a consuming hatred of his brother and wishes to see the end of him.

> The opening scene, in which there is nothing light-hearted or comic, reveals a disturbing background to the comedy that follows. The action starts when Orlando, the younger brother, now grown up but still regarded as a 'boy', decides to assert himself against the oppression of his elder brother. He tells Oliver: 'The spirit of my father grows strong in me, and I will no longer endure it' (I.1.65–6). The complaints of Orlando are shown to be entirely justified. All that Oliver says of the supposed villainy of his brother is in fact true of himself. He is mean-spirited and malicious in his treatment of Orlando, manipulative in his dealings with the well-intentioned

Charles and vicious in his own designs without any good reason or mitigating motivation; as he admits at the end, he simply hates his brother because he is a more attractive person and more popular than himself. Although it is not directly stated, it seems that he would be only too happy to see his brother dead. Shakespeare uses the convention of the soliloquy (in which characters reveal their true thoughts and feelings) twice in this scene to make the wickedness of Oliver absolutely clear.

Within the dynamic framework of the quarrel in the present action we are informed of the trespass of brother against brother in the earlier usurpation of Duke Senior by his younger brother Frederick. No justification is given here or elsewhere in the play other than Frederick's desire for power. It is an artful device to show these two rifts between brothers in parallel and to give the audience essential background information about the usurpation while the rift that involves the male protagonist (Orlando) and his brother is enacted before our eyes. Duke Senior is said to be living the carefree life of the golden age in the Forest of Arden (I.1.112). In classical myth the golden age is a time of innocence like that enjoyed by Adam and Eve in the Biblical story. The opening of the play presents us with a dramatic representation of human wickedness and greed in marked contrast to these idyllic suggestions.

This opening scene establishes the character of Orlando. He is assertive, honest and bold. The tribute to his good character at the end carries special authority coming as it does from the mouth of Oliver in a soliloquy. Of particular note is the remark that he is 'never schooled and yet learned, full of noble device' (I.1.155–6). He is articulate and in sparring with his elder brother he shows that he is adept in the **wordplay** in which the play abounds. Although he proves to be no match for the witty Rosalind later in the play, he has a linguistic intelligence that together with his other qualities of brave independence and honesty makes him a worthy suitor.

2 **bequeathed** the subject *he* (Orlando's father) is to be understood here and before *charged*

4 **breed** educate, bring up

4–5 **My brother Jaques** his only appearance is the final scene; he is not to be confused with the character Jaques who is present throughout the action

5 **keeps at school** maintains at university

6 **keeps me rustically** constrains me here in the country

8 **unkept** uncared for, with a pun on *keeps* (lines 5 and 6)

11 **fair** healthy, handsome

manage movements proper to a trained horse

16 **countenance** demeanour, bearing or style of living

17 **hinds** farm labourers

18–19 **mines my gentility** undermines my noble birth or status

27 **what make you here?** what are you doing here? Orlando's reply puns on *make* = *create*, the **antithesis** of *mar* then taken up by Oliver

33–4 **be naught awhile** be nothing, begone, an insult

36 **prodigal portion** alluding to the proverb of the Prodigal Son (Luke 15: 11–32) who 'wasted' his allotted portion of goods and 'would fain have filled his belly with the husks the swine did eat'

42 **gentle** well-born

42–3 **courtesy of nations** conventions of the civilised world

51 **too young in this** too inexperienced when it comes to wrestling; once again a witty play by Orlando (on younger and older)

53 **I am no villain** there is a pun here on two meanings: wicked and low-born

58 **railed on** insulted

67 **exercises** employment, training

81 **physic your rankness** cure your disease; curb your growth

110 **Robin Hood** the legendary chivalric outlaw of the Middle Ages who lived in Sherwood Forest

111–12 **fleet the time carelessly** pass the time without worries or duties

112 **the golden world** in classical myth, the golden age was a time of innocence, purity and justice before the advent of civilisation and its attendant evils when men lived in harmony with nature and without having to labour

122 **loath to foil him** unwilling to throw him and injure him

131 **underhand** indirect

136 **I had as lief** I would be just as glad if

139 **practise** intrigue or plot against, contrive

145 **anatomise** dissect, analyse

153 **gamester** athlete, idler

SCENE 2 Celia and Rosalind witness Orlando's victory over Charles. Orlando falls in love with Rosalind

Rosalind, daughter of the banished Duke Senior, is comforted by her cousin Celia, daughter of Duke Frederick, who promises that when her father dies, she will return the dukedom to Rosalind. She cheers up and jokes with Celia. Touchstone, the court jester, enters to summon Celia to her father. They indulge in a bout of verbal sparring until the courtier Le Beau enters with news that the wrestler Charles has thrown and seriously injured three young men. The next bout will take place where they are now. Duke Frederick, Charles and Orlando then enter.

At the request of the Duke, who fears for the safety of Charles's opponent, Celia and Rosalind try to dissuade Orlando from entering what seems like such an unequal contest on the grounds of his youth and inexperience. Orlando courteously declines to be persuaded and surprises everyone by throwing his opponent who has to be carried off. The Duke asks Orlando his name. Displeased when he learns he is the son of Sir Rowland who had formerly been his enemy, he brusquely departs. Rosalind, on the contrary, is moved to find that he is the son of a man much loved by her father and gives him the chain she is wearing round her neck, whereupon Orlando is lost for words, recognising that he has been overcome by Rosalind.

Le Beau returns to warn Orlando to leave the place as the moody Duke misconstrues what he has done. Orlando makes enquiries about the young women from Le Beau who tells him that Rosalind too has displeased the Duke for no other reason than her popularity with the people who praise her for her virtues and pity her for her father's sake. Orlando feels caught between a tyrant brother and a tyrant Duke but also enraptured with the heavenly Rosalind.

This scene has great variety in tone, character and action. It starts by introducing the two principal women, with the unfortunate Rosalind in melancholy mood. When Celia bids her be merry, her reply – 'From henceforth I will, coz, and devise sports. Let me see – what do you think of falling in love?' (I.2.23–4) – reveals a character who will deliberately use her **wit** and intelligence to triumph over misfortune; it also encapsulates the sportive spirit of this romantic comedy. The sportive character of the women is intensified with the entry of Touchstone, who is funny in himself and the cause of further humour in the jokes that the witty women can make at his expense. The comedy is diversified with the entry of Le Beau whose formal pomposity makes him a target for the wit of the others. With the entry of the Duke the tone changes, preparing us for the serious business of the scene and its dramatic climax in the wrestling match and the first encounter of Rosalind and Orlando. The serious action in which the unhappy Orlando is in danger but triumphs establishes him as a man of courageous action as the opening scene had shown him to be verbally adept, and therefore a fully worthy suitor of Rosalind.

1 **coz** cousin, also a term of endearment

5 **learn me** teach me

9–10 **so thou hadst been still with me** provided that you had still been with me

12 **righteously tempered** correctly compounded or blended

19 **render thee again in affection** return to you out of love

23 **devise sports** invent diverting entertainments

28 **come off again** extricate yourself

30–1 **mock the good housewife Fortune from her wheel** Fortune was proverbially depicted as a blindfolded woman turning a huge wheel on which people were moved from high to low; here she is belittled by being equated to a housewife with a spinning wheel. Celia means that by virtue of their sport and mirth, they will be able to triumph over their misfortunes and so defeat Fortune's power

37 **honest** chaste

40–1 **Fortune ... Nature** Fortune gives mortals wealth, power and status, but beauty and ugliness are the gifts of Nature

47 **Nature's natural** Nature's idiot referring ironically to Touchstone who enters at this point. He is an intelligent fool, as Celia recognises in calling him 'wit'

52 **whetstone** a stone for sharpening metals, a word that plays on the fool's name: a touchstone tests metals

57 **messenger** not only a bringer of messages but also the official employed to arrest a prisoner

58 **by mine honour** an upper class oath, strictly inappropriate for Touchstone, since only the upper classes had honour

80 **taxation** satire, criticism

87 **the Beu** an anglicised form of the French Le Beau meaning the handsome or the fine: in view of what follows it seems clear that Celia is mocking him

89 **put on us** force down our throats

95 **colour** kind or type, possibly not understood by the Frenchman

98 **Destinies decrees** picking up Rosalind's 'fortune' in mock solemnity. Hence Celia's remark that his phrase is 'laid on with a trowel', that is, repeating the idea with unsubtle emphasis

100 **rank** maintain my high status (by using pompous language). Rosalind interrupts with a pun taking rank to mean 'evil-smelling'

111 **old tale** Celia mocks Le Beau's fairy tale opening

112 **proper** handsome

114–15 **'Be it known unto all men by these presents'** by this present document, a legal phrase, punning on Le Beau's 'presence' and mocking the formality of his language

121 **dole** lamentation

131–2 **broken music** refers to the sound of rib-breaking; part music written for different instruments or voices

132 **dotes upon** is infatuated with

140 **forwardness** rashness

197 **Hercules be thy speed** may Hercules, a great achiever of physical feats in classical myth, be your helper

204–5 **I am not yet well breathed** I am not yet warmed up

217 **a gallant youth** in the Duke's reactions to Orlando before and after he discovers his identity we see the best and worst side of his character

230 **Sticks me at heart** pierces me to the heart

235 **out of suits** out of favour; Rosalind and Orlando are united in misfortune

240 **quintain** a post or block used for tilting practice

241 **He calls us back. My pride fell with my fortunes** Orlando, lost for words, does not call them back. Rosalind offers an excuse for her forwardness in saying that with her loss of position has gone the pride and decorum proper to a princess

254 **misconsters** miscontrues

255 **humorous** moody

261 **taller** elsewhere Rosalind is said to take on male disguise because she is tall

276 **from the smoke into the smother** proverbial, meaning from a bad situation to a worse. A smother is a dense smoke

SCENE 3 Rosalind admits to Celia that she is in love with Orlando. Duke Frederick banishes her from the court

Rosalind is again in gloomy mood as she talks to Celia about her new found love for Orlando. The Duke enters and unceremoniously banishes Rosalind from his court on pain of death if she is found within twenty miles of it after ten days. When asked for a reason, he says that he does not trust her. Rosalind protests innocence of treachery but to no avail. Celia intervenes to point out that since they have been inseparable she too must be a traitor. The Duke calls her a fool; Rosalind is too clever for her, moreover her presence overshadows Celia's, since the people pity her, moved by her very silence and patience. He is determined and repeats the sentence.

After he has left, Celia, loath to be parted from her dearest friend, takes the initiative in her decision to accompany Rosalind in her exile. She suggests that they seek out Rosalind's father in the Forest of Arden. Rosalind thinks of the danger in which the two women would find themselves. Celia suggests that they dress in humble clothes, but it is Rosalind, the taller of the two, who has the idea to disguise herself as a man. She decides on the name Ganymede, while Celia takes the name Aliena. Rosalind then suggests that they take Touchstone with them for comfort and support.

Duke Frederick is revealed in his true colours in this scene. His banishment of Rosalind is motivated by envy of her popularity, fear and malice. He is shown in the same light as Oliver, as a character whose actions reflect the darker side of human nature. By contrast Rosalind, who defends herself with dignity and self control, and Celia who generously vows to share Rosalind's exile, are transparently characters of integrity and worth.

This scene establishes the central dramatic device of disguise. This sportive device is the main source of the comedy that follows but in the plot of the play it is undertaken for serious practical reasons. Although plans for the departure to the Forest of Arden are jointly made, it is Rosalind's idea to dress as a man. On the Elizabethan stage, since women's parts were played by adolescent boys, the disguise would have been easily accomplished

The final line of this first act, in which Celia says they are going not into banishment but to *liberty* highlights one of the play's main themes; the contrast between tyranny and restriction at the court of Duke Frederick and the freedom that can be enjoyed in the Forest of Arden.

1 **Cupid** the Roman god of love

16 **burs** sticky heads of a common plant which children throw at each other for fun

19 **hem** cough

24 **you will try in time** you will have a wrestling match with Orlando

24–5 **in despite of a fall** the wrestling **metaphor** contains a sexual allusion

45 **intelligence** communication

51 **purgation** the action of clearing oneself of guilt

73 **Juno's swans** swans are more usually associated with Venus the goddess of love than Juno the goddess of marriage

78 **she robs thee of thy name** she diminishes your reputation

110 **umber** brown earth used to make pigment

115 **curtle-axe** a short broad cutting sword, a cutlass

118 **swashing** blustering, swaggering

120 **outface it with their semblances** present a bold face to the world in their appearance

123 **Ganymede** a beautiful youth stolen from earth by Jupiter to become his cupbearer

126 **Aliena** alien, other; outcast, alien from her father

ACT II

SCENE 1 In conversation with his lords, Duke Senior extols the merits of life in the Forest of Arden. They tell him how their hunting of the deer upsets the melancholy Jaques. They all set off to find him

In the Forest of Arden, Duke Senior, in the company of Amiens and two lords, extols the virtues of their life away from the pomp and falsity of the court. He then suggests that they go and hunt for venison but expresses regret that in hunting they have to kill the creatures who are natives of the forest. One of his companions then reports the opinion of the melancholy Jaques that the Duke's killing of the deer is more of a usurpation than the supplanting of the Duke by his younger brother. He goes on to tell how he and Amiens spied on Jaques as he beheld a wounded stag on the bank of the neighbouring brook and 'moralized' the spectacle (line 45) into a thousand similes, concluding that the exiled courtiers are mere usurpers and tyrants in their new environment. The Duke asks to be taken to Jaques saying he loves to debate with him when he is in a melancholy mood as he is then full of interesting ideas.

The Duke's opening speech stoically praising the virtues of life in the Forest of Arden in preference to the life at court is central to the debate about values contained in the action of the play. It should be noted that life is the forest is not a wholly ideal state. They are still subject to 'the penalty of Adam' (II.1.5), seasonal change. Nevertheless the Duke finds nature to be an uplifting source of moral teaching. This moralising is continued in slightly melodramatic form in the speech of Jaques on the subject of the killing of the deer. His speech is a reminder that life in the forest is not a paradise; in the classical golden age, nature provided food for man unbidden without the need to kill. As a melancholy character in a sportive comedy, his 'humour' is to some extent out of place. There are hints here that the other courtiers find his determined melancholy a source of amusement.

4 **the envious court** as exemplified in the conduct of Duke Ferdinand and Oliver

5 **Here we feel not the penalty of Adam** here we are none the worse for seasonal change. In Eden before the fall, Adam and Eve lived in an eternal springtime. The experience of winter was part of Adam's punishment for disobeying God

11 **feelingly** by making themselves felt

13 **the toad** supposed to be venomous (poisonous) in Elizabethan times. It was also thought that it had a jewel in its head which had great virtues, one being that it was an antidote to poison

15 **exempt from public haunt** not subject to normal human traffic

19 **translate** transform hardship but also create a sweet discourse about it

22 **fools** innocent, vulnerable creatures

23 **burghers** citizens

24 **forkèd heads** arrows

25 **haunches** hindquarters

26 **The melancholy Jaques** Jaques is a humour character, one whose disposition is governed by an excess of black bile that engenders depression and sullenness

31 **antick** ancient or grotesque

32 **brawls** makes its way noisily over stones

33 **sequestered** separated from the herd

44 **moralize this spectacle** make the scene the subject of moral reflection

46 **needless** having no need of further water

47 **testament** as in last will and testament

50 **velvet friend** referring to the deer but also suggesting smooth-coated courtiers, fair-weather friends

51–2 **doth part / The flux of company** does separate the flood of people

58 **invectively** satirically

67 **cope him** match wits with him

SCENE 2 Duke Frederick sends for Oliver to help him find Celia and Rosalind whom he believes to be in the company of Orlando

In conversation with his lords, Duke Frederick, who has discovered that Celia and Rosalind are missing, cannot believe that they left without the knowledge and help of someone at his court. One of the lords reports that the women were much taken with Orlando and speculates that he is in their company. The Duke orders that he be sent for and that if he is missing that Oliver be brought to him so that he can order him to search for his brother.

8 **roynish** coarse, scurvy

17 **that gallant** Orlando

20 **inquisition quail** investigation fail or slacken

SCENE 3 Adam warns Orlando of Oliver's plot against his life. Together they leave Oliver's house

Orlando's faithful servant Adam laments the ghastliness of a world in which men's virtues can work to their disadvantage by making them envied and warns Orlando that he has overheard Oliver, envious of the praise he has won for his courage in the wrestling match, planning to burn down his lodging with him inside. He advises Orlando not to enter his brother's house. Orlando replies that he has not the means to live elsewhere and rather than be a beggar or a thief will risk the malice of his brother. Adam offers him the five hundred crowns he has saved for his old age and asks him to take him as his servant. Orlando is moved by his loyalty and decides to seek a new life of modest means, taking Adam with him.

This scene offers a moving example of true loyalty and service in the concern shown for Orlando by Adam and in the reciprocal feeling of Orlando.

4 **what make you here?** what are you doing here?

7 **fond** foolish

8 **bonny prizer** fine prize-fighter

11 **graces** virtues that grace them

23 **you use to lie** are wont to lie

37 **diverted blood** a blood relationship taking an unnatural course

39 **thrifty hire** wages thriftily saved

43 **He that doth the ravens feed** a Biblical reference. God feeds the ravens at Psalm 147:9 and is said to show concern for the sparrows in Matthew 10:29

50 **with unbashful forehead** brazenly; evidently a reference to sexual abstinence

65 **In lieu of** in return for

68 **low content** humble contentment

74 **too late a week** far too late

SCENE 4 Rosalind, Celia and Touchstone overhear Silvius talking to Corin of his love for Phebe. They make arrangements for Corin to buy his master's flock, pasture and cottage where they propose to live

In the Forest of Arden, Rosalind disguised as Ganymede, Celia disguised as Aliena and Touchstone, weary after their journey, come upon two shepherds, the aged Corin and the young Silvius. They overhear Silvius talking in extravagant terms of his love for Phebe. Rosalind recognises in the emotions of Silvius something of her own condition and Touchstone recalls his love for one Jane Smile. Celia bids Touchstone ask Corin if they can buy food from him. Corin replies courteously but says he works for a mean master who is not disposed to give hospitality and in any case as everything he owns is currently up for sale there is no food available. Rosalind asks who is going to buy the flock and the pasture. Corin replies that they will go to Silvius 'that little cares for buying anything' (II.4.87) Rosalind then proposes that Corin buy the cottage, the pasture and the flock with money from the travellers. Celia promises to improve his wages. Corin invites them to further inspection and promises that if they like what they see he will buy it with their gold and be their 'very faithful feeder' (II.4.96). (This scene to line 72 is examined in Textual Analysis.)

Rosalind who is in love herself overhears the shepherd Silvius talking romantically of his love for the disdainful Phebe. What might have been a purely **pastoral** interlude is modified by two factors: the bawdy and very unromantic perspective of Touchstone and the realistic presentation of the economic situation in which the dependent Corin finds himself.

1 **Jupiter** in Roman myth, the king of the gods and master of Ganymede

6 **the weaker vessel** woman; the phrase is Biblical in origin deriving from 1 Peter 3:7

doublet-and-hose the tight-fitting jacket and breeches worn by Elizabethan gentlemen

7 **petticoat** typifying femininity

10 **bear no cross** **wordplay** meaning carry no burden and have no money (some Elizabethan coins bore crosses)

27 **fantasy** fancy, object of desire

40 **searching of** examining, probing

41 **hard adventure** painful experience

45 **batler** a laundry club used to beat clothes in the wash

46 **chopt** chapped

47 **peascod** peapod; lovers wooed with peapods. As 'cods' is slang for testicles and 'wear' slang for sexual intercourse, this whole passage doubtless has a bawdy meaning

51 **mortal in folly** subject to the promptings of appetite and the passions, irrational

52 **ware of** aware; also careful in avoiding

61 **you clown** you rustic or yokel; Touchstone addresses the countryman as his inferior for which he is put in his place by Rosalind

78 **little recks** little cares

80 **cote** small cottage

bounds of feed tracts of pasture

88 **if it stand with honesty** if it is compatible with fair dealing (as far as Silvius is concerned)

90 **to pay for it of us** receive what you need to pay for it from us

92 **waste** spend, pass

96 **feeder** servant or shepherd

SCENE 5 An interlude in which Amiens sings, Jaques elicits from him a second verse and adds one of his own

Amiens sings a verse of 'Under the greenwood tree'. Jaques cajoles him into singing another verse. When Amiens tells him that the Duke has been looking for him all day, Jaques replies that he has been avoiding him all day because he finds him too argumentative. He gives Amiens a third verse that he has composed himself. Amiens goes off to find the Duke, as food has been prepared for him. (This scene and the next are examined in Textual Analysis.)

The sweet song of Amiens praises the life of nature, free from ambition; it sustains the pastoral note and the idyllic associations of life in the Forest of Arden. However, the conversation of the cynical Jaques and his own verse mocking those who leave wealth and ease strikes a contrary note just as the clowning of Touchstone prevents the theme of romantic love from becoming cloying. A balance of attitudes is therefore being perpetually struck throughout the play which seldom settles unambiguously to one view.

3 **turn** shape, form

14 **ragged** rough, harsh

16 **stanzo** stanza, verse

24 **dog-apes** baboons

25–6 **renders me the beggarly thanks** gives me thanks in return, which befits a beggar

32 **disputable** argumentative

36 **live i'th'sun** live outdoors, live a carefree life

44 **in despite of my invention** even though I have little imagination or in spite of my poetic powers

51 **Ducdame** pronounced with three syllables, a nonsensical word

58 **the first-born of Egypt** a Biblical reference: when the Israelites fled from their captivity in Egypt, God killed the eldest child in every Egyptian family (Exodus 12:29)

SCENE 6 Arrived in the Forest, Orlando comforts the weary Adam and promises to bring him food

Faint for lack of nourishment, Adam tells Orlando that he can go no further. Orlando vows to search the forest for food. He carries Adam to a place of shelter. (This scene together with the previous scene is discussed in Textual Analysis.)

A further perspective on life in the forest is offered by this scene; it is inhospitable to strangers, a wild and deserted place where the air is 'bleak' (II.6.14). In this setting the decent humanity of Orlando stands out.

6 **uncouth** wild, uncivilised

7 **conceit** imagination

9 **comfortable** comforted, at ease

10 **presently** shortly

13 **Well said** well done. Orlando is presumably responding to a gesture from Adam

16 **desert** wild place

scene 7 Jaques tells of his meeting with Touchstone. Orlando interrupts to demand food. When the Duke offers this willingly, he departs to fetch Adam. Jaques discourses on the seven ages of man. Orlando enters with Adam. They eat, are entertained with a song and welcomed to the company of the Duke

Duke Senior is still looking for Jaques when he enters in a state of excitement announcing that he has met a fool (Touchstone) in the forest. He reports the fool's moral observations on the passage of time which have greatly amused him. He envies the fool's profession, saying that he wants to wear the fool's garb himself. When the Duke agrees, Jaques makes it clear that he wishes for the liberty traditionally accorded to the fool to speak his mind and 'Cleanse the foul body of th'infected world' (II.7.60). The Duke then accuses him of hypocrisy, alleging that he has been a notorious libertine himself. Jaques then says that since sin is so general no one will be especially singled out for attack; it will be a case of: if the cap fits, wear it.

Their conversation is abruptly interrupted by the entry of Orlando who demands that the assembled company stop eating until 'necessity be served' (II.7.90). He threatens to kill anyone who touches the food till his needs are met. When the Duke welcomes him and speaks courteously to him, he apologises saying that he supposed in such a remote place hard words would be necessary. Then in an eloquent speech he appeals to their sense of compassion and puts away his sword. The Duke readily responds. Orlando then asks them to wait while he goes to fetch his faithful servant, weighed down by age and hunger. After he has gone, the Duke remarks that they are not alone in their misfortune 'This wide and universal theatre / Presents more woeful pageants than the scene / Wherein we play in' (II.7.138–40). At this point Jaques delivers the most famous speech of the play on the seven ages of man 'All the world's a stage, / And all the men and women merely players'. Orlando returns carrying Adam. They eat while Amiens sings 'Blow, blow, thou winter wind' (II.7.175). In the course of the song Orlando has revealed his identity to the Duke who after it is finished bids him a hearty welcome which he extends also to Adam bidding them go to his cave where he may learn the rest of their story.

This is Jaques's biggest scene; he dominates it at the beginning and the end. His reaction to his meeting with Touchstone in the forest is slightly manic. What the fool says is hardly worth an hour's laughter. Nevertheless, although they are opposite in temperament and humour, Jaques and Touchstone share a somewhat jaundiced attitude to the world and he recognises something of his own alienation in Touchstone's **wit**. Intriguing is the Duke's opinion, which is neither confirmed nor contradicted by anything in the rest of the play, that Jaques has been a notorious libertine and therefore is in no position to assume the role of censorious scourge in criticising the rest of the world. Jaques, in his defence of the liberty he wishes to assume in his imagined role as fool, does not deny what the Duke has said. He merely asserts that he will only attack vices generally. Although the Duke's judgement might be thought to undermine the integrity of Jaques, Shakespeare gives him the longest and most serious speech of the play on the theme of the seven ages of man.

5 **compact of jars** made up of discords (compare with a jarring note)
musical the Duke uses music as a **metaphor** for inner harmony
6 **discord in the spheres** alluding to the widely held theory that the earth was surrounded by eight concentric crystalline spheres in which moved the planets and the stars. Their orderly movement produced a harmonious music
13 **motley** the parti-coloured dress of the professional fool
17 **set terms** with severity
19 **fool ... fortune** a reference to the proverb 'God sends fortune to fools.
20 **dial from his poke** watch from his bag
23 **wags** goes on
26–8 **hour ... ripe ... tale** perhaps there is a bawdy undercurrent here, 'hour' suggesting whore, 'rot' suggesting venereal disease and 'tale' suggesting tail, the male sexual organ
29 **moral** moralise
30 **Chanticleer** the stock name for a cock in medieval and Renaissance times
32 **sans intermission** without interruption
38–9 **brain ... dry** a dry brain preserved a good memory and housed a dry wit

39 **remainder biscuit** ship's biscuits left over

41–2 **he vents / In mangled forms** he utters in twisted language; for self protection the professional fool disguised his wisdom and censure by mixing it with apparent nonsense

45 **suit** request; set of clothes

55 **senseless of the bob** aware of the sting or rebuke of the fool's jest

57 **squandering glances** widely scattered satirical taunts

63 **counter** token

66 **brutish sting** animal lust

67 **embossèd** swollen

headed evils evils that have come to a head like a boil, possibly suggesting the sores of venereal disease

71 **tax any private party** criticise any single individual; this is the stock defence of the satirist that he only attacks vices in general

80 **bravery** finery, splendid clothes

82 **mettle** spirit

85 **free** innocent

86 **taxing** criticism

95 **You touched my vein at first** you were right with your first suggestion

97 **inland bred** having refinement, not outlandish

126 **take upon command** take simply by asking for it

151 **like the pard** like the leopard

157 **wise saws and modern instances** wise sayings and commonplace examples

159 **pantaloon** foolish old man, a popular stock character in Italian comedy

161 **hose** breeches

162 **shank** thigh

197 **effigies** likeness

198 **limned** painted

ACT III

SCENE 1 Duke Frederick charges Oliver with the task of bringing back Orlando dead or alive within a year or face exile

Duke Frederick hints that he has considered taking revenge on Oliver and orders him to bring Orlando to him dead or alive within a year or face exile. In the meantime his lands and property are to be forfeited. Oliver tells the Duke that he never loved his brother. This confession does not win the favour of the Duke who gives orders that Oliver be expelled from his house.

> This brief scene makes a dramatic contrast in tone and mood from the previous and next scenes set in the forest.

3 **argument** object
6 **Seek him with candle** look into every dark corner
7 **turn** return
11 **quit thee** prove yourself innocent
18 **Make an extent** begin with legal action
19 **turn him going** send him on his way

SCENE 2 Orlando pins up verses on the forest trees. Corin and Touchstone debate the merits of life in the country and the court. Rosalind finds and reads one of Orlando's poems. Touchstone parodies it. Celia enters with another and discloses their author to Rosalind. They overhear Orlando in conversation with Jaques. Rosalind, maintaining her disguise as Ganymede, persuades Orlando to woo her as if she were his Rosalind in order to cure him of his love

Orlando, alone on stage, declares his intention to hang verses on the forest's trees and to carve them in their barks. Corin and Touchstone argue about the respective merits of life in the forest and life at court and about the manners appropriate to each. Rosalind enters reading one of Orlando's love poems addressed anonymously to her. It is immediately parodied by Touchstone. Celia enters and reads another of Orlando's poems. She then dismisses Corin and Touchstone so that she can disclose to Rosalind that Orlando is the author of the verses for she has seen him swooning beneath an oak tree. When Orlando and Jaques then enter, Rosalind and Celia withdraw to observe their conversation in which Orlando gets the better of Jaques in witty banter culminating on the topics of folly and love. Jaques departs. Rosalind (still in her disguise) decides to accost Orlando and speak to him 'like a saucy lackey' (III.2.287).

Rosalind engages Orlando on a discourse on time in which she alludes to the way in which time passes for the lover. He is intrigued by her accent in which he detects something refined. She replies that she was taught to speak by an old religious uncle, 'one that knew courtship too well' (III.2.333) and spoke against it charging women with many giddy offences. When Orlando asks her to specify these, she refuses, saying 'I will not cast away my physic but to those that are sick' (III.2.344–5), such as the man who abuses the forest trees by carving on them the name 'Rosalind'; he is one who deserves her good counsel. Orlando confesses that he is that man, but Rosalind says that he exhibits none of the true signs of the lover. When Orlando protests a true love that neither rhyme nor reason can express, Rosalind call love 'merely a madness' (III.2.383) and offers to cure it by counsel, claiming to have cured such a lover by having him woo her as his mistress whereupon she drove him into a real madness by feigning a giddy changefulness that made him renounce the world. Orlando says that he does not want to be cured, but when Rosalind offers to cure him if he will come daily to her cottage and woo her as if she were his 'Rosalind', he agrees.

Centrally placed at a mid point in the action this scene is the longest in the play and the first of three (the others being IV.1 and V.2) in which the disguised Rosalind talks to and courts Orlando.

At the outset Orlando appears in the typical pose of the courtly lover, writing verses to his beloved. However this typical pose is undercut by the mockery of the women and the cynical **wit** of Touchstone who, as a proponent of courtly manners in his debate with Corin, puts the pose of courtliness in a ridiculous light. His parody of the verses further supplements the women's mockery of Orlando's poor verse. In this scene as in the whole play, wit, which may be defined here as a playful intelligence, triumphs at the expense of traditional poetic **romance** represented by the clichéd style of Orlando's courtly verse. Orlando, though, is not made to look a complete fool; he is able to get the better of Jaques in their wit-combat; the defeat and departure of 'Monsieur Melancholy' (III.2. 286) at this juncture as the spirits of the principal characters rise is fitting and has symbolic effect. Orlando is then outdazzled himself by the wit of Rosalind who further ridicules the affectation of the male courtier and brilliantly manipulates him into seeking a cure for his madness. The romantic encounter between the lovers begins, therefore, most unromantically; traditional courtship is shown to be a rather silly game and Shakespeare's plot allows an intelligent woman to turn the tables on the conventional male behaviour.

2 **thrice-crownèd queen of night** the moon, in classical myth the goddess reigned as Selene (Luna in Latin) in heaven, Artemis (Diana) the huntress on earth and Persephone (Proserpina) in the underworld

3 **chaste** Diana was the goddess of chastity

4 **Thy huntress' name** Rosalind, disguised as a huntress

6 **character** inscribe, write

10 **unexpressive she** inexpressible, indescribable woman

16 **private** given to privation or deprivation

18 **spare** lacking in luxury, austere

28 **complain of good breeding** complain of not having been born or brought up well

30 **a natural philosopher** wordplay: a scientist or a philosopher who is a fool

39 **manners** two meanings are played upon by Touchstone: etiquette or morals

49 **instance** provide proof

50 **fells** fleeces

61 **civet** a musky perfume derived from the glands in the anus of the civet cat

62 **worm's meat** food for worms

64 **perpend** consider

65 **flux** discharge

76 **bawd** procurer or pimp

bell-wether the leading sheep of the flock around whose neck a bell was hung

78 **cuckoldy** the horns of the ram could also serve as an emblem of a cuckold (the victim of adultery)

84 **western Ind** West Indies

94 **right butter-women's rank to market** like a series of women taking their butter to market; Touchstone is commenting adversely on the quality of the rhymes

97 **hart ... hind** the female and male deer

99 **after kind** act like one of its own kind, seek one of its own kind

101 **lined** have a lining (for warmth in winter); lined also has bawdy associations referring to the copulation of dogs

103 **sheaf** gather cut stalks of corn into bundles

104 **cart** refers to a farm cart but brings to mind the carts behind which whores and bawds were driven through the streets in public punishment

108 **prick** thorn (as of a rose), the male sexual organ

109 **false gallop** tedious canter. Touchstone is parodying the monotonous regularity of Orlando's verses

113 **graff** graft

114 **medlar** the fruit of the medlar-tree, with a pun on *meddler*; meddle can also mean to engage in sexual activity

124 **civil** civilised

127 **span** the distance from the tip of the thumb to the tip of the little finger

128 **Buckles in** holds, encloses

136 **in little** in miniature

141 **Helen** in Greek myth, the most beautiful woman in the world; her abduction (not exactly unwilling) at the hands of Paris caused the Trojan War

142 **Cleopatra** queen of Egypt; the most famous female ruler of the ancient world whose seductive charm overcame Julius Caesar and then Mark Antony

143 **Atalanta's better part** in Greek myth, a beautiful maiden who excelled in running and sought to remain chaste by refusing to marry anyone who could not beat her in a foot race. Failure to win entailed death for her suitors. Her better part is presumably her chaste beauty as opposed to her cruelty

144 **Lucretia** in Roman legend, the wife of Collatinus who was raped by Tarquin, son of the last king of Rome. She killed herself rather than endure the shame

157 **bag and baggage** indicates that an army withdraws honourably having time to take all its possession with it

158 **scrip and scrippage** a scrip is a small wallet or bag

161 **feet** metrical feet

169 **seven of the nine days** referring to a the novelty of a 'nine day's wonder'; Rosalind is saying that she has been wondering for some time already

171 **Pythagoras** a Greek philosopher who believed in the reincarnation of the soul and its transmigration through the various species

172 **Irish rat** the Irish were believed to kill of rats through the recitation of poems

173 **Trow** do you know?

186–7 **out of all whooping!** beyond what can be expressed by exclamations

191 **a South Sea of discovery** as long and frustrating as a voyage to the South seas

197 **put a man in your belly** a bawdy meaning suggested by 'drinking', having sexual intercourse

218 **Gargantua's mouth** Gargantua is one of the giants who features in the Renaissance comic satire of Rabelais *Gargantua and Pantagruel*

221 **catechism** a summary of the principles of the Christian faith made in the form of question and answer

225 **atomies** specks, motes

229 **Jove's tree** the oak tree was sacred to Jupiter (Jove) in Roman myth

237 **'holla'** halt, a command used to a horse

curvets leaps, frisks about

239 **heart** punning on 'hart', a female deer

240 **burden** refrain, also referring to Rosalind's interruption

257 **Yes, just** yes, exactly

264 **goldsmith's wives** Jaques is suggesting that Orlando has learned ('conned') his verses from the mottoes inscribed on the inside of gold rings

266 **I answer you painted cloths** cheap wall hangings adorned with pictures and sometimes mottoes; I answer you plainly

269 **Atalanta's heels** the famous athlete, see above

282 **cipher** the figure o, a thing of no value

287 **a saucy lackey** an impudent page

306 **se'nnight** week

327 **coney** rabbit

333 **courtship** courtliness, wooing

349 **fancy-monger** a dealer in love

350 **quotidian** fever recurring every day

355–6 **cage of rushes** a cage easily broken out of

358 **blue** that is, with dark rings under the eyes

359 **unquestionable** not submitting to questions, impatient

367 **point-device in your accoutrements** precise in your dress

374 **still** always

392 **moonish** changeable

403 **wash your liver as clean** the liver was regarded as the seat of the passions

SCENE 3 Touchstone talks to Audrey whom he has decided to marry. When the vicar arrives to perform the ceremony, Jaques persuades Touchstone to marry in church

In the presence of Jaques, Touchstone courts the goat-herd Audrey and declares his intention to marry her despite her ugliness. A country vicar, Sir Oliver Martext, who has been summoned by Touchstone to marry them in the forest enters to do so, but Jaques persuades Touchstone to marry in church.

Touchstone's earthy and distinctly ungallant wooing of Audrey together with his cynical view of marriage make a comic contrast with what has just passed in the previous scene in which the love relationship between Rosalind and Orlando begins to develop.

6 **capricious** goatish, derived from the Latin *caper* 'goat', suggesting friskiness and perhaps lasciviousness. The Roman poet Ovid, author of a famous and risqué verse treatise called *The Art of Love*, was banished from Rome for some unknown reason by the emperor Augustus to Pontus on the shores of the Black Sea; rumour had it that he had seduced the emperor's daughter Julia. Touchstone's classical allusions are wasted upon Audrey
honest in view of the above story which Shakespeare must have known, honest must be used in an ironic sense, or possibly just means well-born. Like so much of what Touchstone says, the utterance is teasingly ambiguous

7 **Goths** an uncivilised people who dwelt on the shores of the Black Sea; pronounced to rhyme with goats in Elizabethan times

8 **ill-inhabited** inappropriately housed (in Touchstone)

8–9 **Jove in a thatched house** Jove, the king of the gods; the allusion is to the story that when Jupiter disguised himself as an ordinary mortal the only people to give him hospitality were a poor old couple called Baucis and Philemon who lived in a humble cottage with a thatched roof (see Ovid's *Metamorphoses*)

11 **seconded with** supported by

12–13 **a great reckoning in a little room** a bill disproportionately large for a small room

18 **feigning** make-believe, pretend

26 **hard-favoured** ugly

29 **material** full of matter, or unspiritual

35 **foul** ugly or morally corrupt

39 **Martext** a tell-tale name, 'spoil text', a comic priest, perhaps a Puritan; there is the possibility of much visual comedy at his expense

45 **stagger** hesitate

46 **horn-beasts** cattle or sheep with horns; horns were the emblem of the cuckold

52 **rascal** poorest deer in the herd

70 **toy** a trifle (referring to the marriage ceremony and perhaps Audrey herself)

72 **the ox hath his bow** the ox has his yoke; Touchstone's argument is that marriage is a kind of servitude that is necessary to hold man's desires in check

79 **wainscot** wood panelling

80 **green timber** unseasoned wood

96 **fantastical** odd, irrational, frivolous

SCENE 4 Rosalind, upset that Orlando has not turned up for their meeting, discusses him with Celia. Corin offers to show them true love being rejected by proud disdain

Rosalind is upset that Orlando has not kept his appointment. She and Celia discuss Orlando's character as a lover and as a man. Corin, who has been repeatedly asked by Rosalind about Silvius, enters and offers to show them the young shepherd in 'a pageant truly played' (III.4.47) being rejected by his proud disdainful beloved. Rosalind says that they will go and watch and that she will play a part in their drama.

When Orlando is on stage, the disguised Rosalind is masterly and controlled. In this scene, by contrast, when she is speaking to Celia as a woman in love, she is exhibits herself some of the giddiness that she has humorously attributed previously to fickle females. Celia, not yet a lover herself, pours scorn on the apparent folly of Orlando.

6 **dissembling** deceiving, perhaps, in view of what follows, because it is reddish-brown (neither one colour nor the other). Red hair is associated with Judas Iscariot, the betrayer of Christ

8 **Judas's children** his kisses are insincere; Judas betrayed Jesus with a kiss

13 **holy bread** bread blessed by the priest for communion

Scene 4 continued

23 **concave** hollow

28 **tapster** barman

38 **quite traverse** obliquely, a reference to an unskilful or cowardly move in knightly combat; knights were supposed to fight straight from the front

39 **puisny tilter** a puny jouster

scene 5 Phebe pitilessly scorns the courtship of Silvius. Rosalind who has observed this intervenes to rebuke her. Phebe is immediately attracted to the disguised Rosalind and is rejected and chided in return. Phebe melts a little towards Silvius and he agrees to deliver a letter to Rosalind

Silvius begs Phebe not to reject him. Rosalind, Celia and Corin enter unobserved to hear Phebe wilfully taking Silvius's love language literally and so turning it to scorn. Silvius replies that if ever Phebe feels the attraction of an appealing face, she will know the pangs of love. As Phebe shows no pity for Silvius, the disguised Rosalind intervenes and rebukes her for insulting and exulting over the wretched, particularly inexplicable for one who has no beauty. As Phebe gazes at him/her, Rosalind warns her not to have any hopes for success with him. She rebukes Silvius for his folly in following such as Phebe and tells Phebe that given her lack of attractiveness she is lucky to have the love of a good man like Silvius. Smitten with the sight of Ganymede, Phebe replies that she had rather hear him chide than Silvius woo. Rosalind rejects Phebe, invites Silvius to her cottage and tells him to press his suit with Phebe.

As Rosalind departs, Phebe finds the truth of the saying 'Who ever loved that loved not at first sight' (III.5.82). Her own plight makes her feel pity for Silvius; she says again that she does not love him but she ceases to reject his companionship and says she will employ him to bear a letter to the person to whom she has just felt attraction. Silvius, no longer completely scorned, is happy to oblige.

Touchstone's lack of gallantry in the previous scene is outdone by Phebe's heartlessness in this scene which makes a further contrast with the romantic relationship that is growing between the principals. Phebe is an incarnation of the disdainful **Petrarchan** mistress, prominent in very many Renaissance sonnets. In taking Silvius's extravagant love language literally she reveals its absurdity. Rosalind is again in control. Her chiding gives Phebe a taste of her own medicine. The ironies of unrequited love are intensified to the point of comic absurdity when Phebe falls for the disguised Rosalind.

1 **Phebe** her name is in Greek an epithet of Artemis (the Roman Diana) the goddess of chastity and hunting

13 **Who shut their coward gates on atomies** who shut their eyelids against specks of dust

23 **The cicatrice and capable impressure** mark and impression received

42–3 **ordinary / Of nature's sale-work** nature's most common and inexpensive ready-made merchandise

44 **tangle** entangle

47 **bugle** dark, black

50 **south** south wind

51 **properer** more handsome, attractive

61 **Cry the man mercy** beg forgiveness of him

69 **sauce** rebuke smartly

73 **vows made in wine** vows made when drunk

76 **ply her hard** press her with all vigour

81 **Dead Shepherd** Shakespeare's predecessor Christopher Marlowe (1564–93). The 'saw' (saying) Phebe quotes is from his narrative poem *Hero and Leander*

89 **extermined** ended, destroyed

108 **carlot** peasant churl

123 **mingled damask** variegated red

133 **omittance is no quittance** failure to do something at the given time does not mean that it will not be done later

ACT IV

SCENE 1 Jaques and Rosalind talk about melancholia. Orlando comes in and the disguised Rosalind bids him woo her as previously agreed. He does so and they go through a mock marriage. Orlando departs and Rosalind confess her love for him

Jaques and Rosalind discuss melancholy and its causes and effects. Orlando enters and greets Rosalind who chides him for being an hour late. He apologises, but his lateness gives Rosalind material to exercise her **wit** at his expense. She bids him woo her. She rejects his suit whereupon Orlando says that he will die. The witty Rosalind argues that in reality no one has ever died for love. She then says she will be more forthcoming and bids Orlando to ask her what he wishes. He proposes marriage. Rosalind asks Celia to marry them and they mimic the marriage ceremony. She then paints an unflattering picture of marriage. Orlando announces that he must go to attend the Duke at dinner and be absent for two hours. Rosalind warns him not to be late back by one minute or she will think him untrustworthy. After Orlando has departed, Celia chides Rosalind for going beyond the usual bounds in her love-talk and says that it is time to unmask her disguise so that the world may see how she has slandered women. Rosalind confesses that she is wholly in love with Orlando and cannot bear to be out of his company.

The genial and gentle mockery of Jaques by Rosalind, resulting in another defeat for him, represents the banishment of melancholy by the mirthful spirit of comedy incarnated in the youthful and optimistic figure of its central character.

This is the second great scene in which the central device of disguise is used to advance the love plot as Rosalind ('in a holiday humour' – IV.1.61) bids Orlando woo her as his lover. In her manipulation of Orlando and in her language, some of which has bawdy undertones, Rosalind is bold, assertive and daring, prompting in Celia the rebuke (after Orlando has left the stage) 'You have simply misused our sex in your love-prate' (IV.1.186–7). The normal conventions in relations between the sexes are subverted through the device of disguise.

16 **simples** ingredients

30 **lisp** speak with an affected foreign accent

42 **Cupid hath clapped him o'th'shoulder** this probably means that Love has only tapped him on the shoulder not seriously affected him

43 **heart-whole** with his emotions intact, unengaged

49 **jointure** property held for the joint use of husband and wife

60 **leer** face, appearance

67 **gravelled for lack of matter** stuck for lack of anything to say

68 **out** at a loss for words

74 **Who could be out?** Who could be at a loss for words? Rosalind in reply takes 'out' punningly to mean 'not engaged in sexual intercourse'

87 **videlicet** that is to say

88 **Troilus** the young son of Priam who was betrayed by Cressida and killed by Achilles

90 **Leander** he used to swim across the Hellespont, the narrow stretch of water between Europe and Asia where the Black Sea meets the Aegean, to visit his beloved Hero who live on the other side and was drowned one night in a storm

127 **your commission** your authority for taking me

139 **Barbary cock-pigeon** traditionally believed to be extremely jealous, this fancy pigeon was introduced into Europe from North Africa

142 **Diana in the fountain** often a centrepiece of a fountain, suitable here because she is the goddess of chastity

144 **hyen** hyena

150 **Make the doors** shut the doors

155 **'Wit, whither wilt?'** proverbial expression addressed to a person whose tongue is running away with him

162 **her husband's occasion** an opportunity to put her husband in the wrong

193 **Bay of Portugal** the sea off the coast of Portugal is deeper than Elizabethan sailors were able to sound

196–8 **bastard of Venus ... that blind rascally boy** Cupid, the son of Venus, was traditionally represented as blind

201 **shadow** place in the shade

SCENE 2 Jaques elicits a song from a forester who has killed a deer that they propose to present to the Duke

Jaques speaks to the lord who has killed the deer and suggests that they present it to the Duke with due ceremony. He bids the forester sing an appropriate song.

It is the function of this interlude to fill in the time demanded by the plot (two hours have to pass before Orlando returns to Rosalind). Jaques, who had earlier lamented at length the killing of the deer in the forest (II.1.27ff), appears to show no disapproval here. The proposal to present the Duke with the deer's horns enables the old joke about cuckoldry, which is a recurrent theme taken up by Touchstone and Rosalind, to be repeated again.

4–5 **deer's horns upon his head** another reference to cuckoldry

5 **branch of victory** like the laurel branch which was a token of victory in the Roman world

13 **burden** refrain

scene 3 Rosalind receives from Silvius a love letter from Phebe. Oliver enters and explains why Orlando has not kept his promise to return within two hours

Rosalind remarks that it is past two o'clock, the hour at which Orlando was due. Silvius enters with Phebe's letter for Rosalind, saying he does not know the contents but suspects from what Phebe has told him (III.5.139) that it will be waspish. Rosalind pretends that it is so, and accuses Silvius of having written it. This he fervently denies. Rosalind then reads the letter which proves to be a confession of love to the bewilderment of the perplexed Silvius. Rosalind rebukes Silvius for loving a woman who will so exploit him and bids him return to her and say that if she loves him [Rosalind] he bids her love Silvius. If she will not, he will not have her unless Silvius pleads on her behalf.

Oliver enters making enquiries about the dwelling in which Rosalind and Celia are living. Celia replies that there is no one at home at present. Oliver finds that the pair fit the description he has been given and asks Ganymede if he is the youth that Orlando calls his 'Rosalind' to whom Orlando commends himself and gives a bloody napkin. Asked to explain himself, Oliver tells how Orlando, returning to keep his appointment, caught sight of a dishevelled man sleeping beneath a tree about whose neck a green snake lay entwined, about to strike his mouth. Seeing Orlando the snake slid off beneath a bush under which a lioness crouched. Orlando then recognised the man as his brother and at first decided to leave him there as food for the lioness. But good nature getting the better of the instinct for revenge he quickly killed the lioness. Oliver is revealed as the brother who has been converted from his evil ways by his brother's generosity. Orlando had led him to the Duke where he revealed an injury to his arm caused by the lioness. He faints with loss of blood, calling upon Rosalind. Oliver binds him up and he recovers his strength, sending Oliver to tell his story and give the reason for his broken promise. Rosalind then faints. When Oliver comments that Rosalind lacks a man's heart, she claims, not very convincingly, that she had been play-acting. They return home.

> Rosalind's pretence, though her intentions are not malicious, compounds the distress of Silvius who is treated quite severely, even tormented.
>
> Oliver's account of his conversion through the generosity of his brother provides further evidence of the essential goodness of Orlando who is not so perfect that he did not contemplate revenge. Oliver's account of Orlando 'Chewing the food of sweet and bitter fancy' (IV.3.102) cleverly introduces what is a fanciful bitter-sweet narrative. The climax of the scene, in which Rosalind faints, is the occasion of comic and touching irony and an indication that under the pressure of her feelings her disguise is beginning to crack.

15 **swaggerer** blusterer

18 **phoenix** a mythical bird of which there was only one alive at any one time

26 **freestone-coloured hand** a brownish hand

34 **Like Turk to Christian** in the Renaissance the Turks were frequently represented as warlike and fierce and after the sack of Constantinople in 1453 as the inveterate enemies of Christendom

36 **Ethiop** black; written in ink; they are black in appearance but even blacker in their meaning

51 **eyne** eyes, a poetical form

77 **purlieus** confines

78 **olive trees** an indication that Arden is essentially a place of fantasy; there are no olive trees in either the Forest of Arden in Warwickshire or in the Ardennes in northern France

79 **neighbour bottom** next dale

80 **rank of osiers** row of willow trees

102 **fancy** love

113 **indented** zigzagging

123 **unnatural** excessively cruel or wicked

132 **hurtling** conflict

141 **recountments** tales

Act V

Scene 1 Touchstone disposes of one of Audrey's suitors, the clown William

Touchstone reassures Audrey that they will soon be married and asks her about the youth in the forest, William, a country bumpkin, who lays claim to her. She denies that he has any claim upon her. When William enters, Touchstone takes pleasure in cross-examining him. He presses his own claim and threatens him, dismissing him from their company. Corin summons Touchstone to his master and mistress.

> Touchstone's treatment of the dim-witted William contrasts with the good-humoured dismissal of Jaques and the disinterested schooling of Silvius by Rosalind. In performance, it may be played as farce, if William is exaggeratedly simple or it may be represented as genuinely threatening. In either case, it serves to enhance the good-natured **wit** and character of Rosalind by contrast.

3–4 **the old gentleman** Jaques who had persuaded Touchstone to marry in church

8 **interest in me** legal concern in, right or title to possession

12 **flouting** jeering, mocking

hold hold back, refrain

30 **'The fool doth think he is wise'** this was the contention of Socrates

42 **ipse** Latin pronoun meaning 'he himself'; here referring to the lover

53 **bastinado** cudgelling

Scene 2 Oliver and Aliena have fallen in love and their marriage is proposed for the following day. Rosalind promises to arrange for Orlando to marry his Rosalind then too. Phebe chides Rosalind for revealing the contents of her letter. Rosalind intimates that the next day will see a general resolution

In conversation between the two brothers it emerges that Oliver and Aliena [Celia] have fallen instantly in love and propose to get married. Oliver declares that he will settle Sir Rowland's estate upon Orlando and live and die a shepherd. Orlando gives his consent. Rosalind and

Orlando briefly discuss the wound to Orlando and Rosalind's pretended swoon before Rosalind confirms the sudden mutual love affair between Oliver and Aliena. Orlando announces that they will be married tomorrow and remarks how bitter it is to look into happiness through another man's eyes. Rosalind then asks him to believe her when she says that she can do strange things and bring about his marriage to Rosalind at the same time. She bids him prepare for marriage the following day.

Phebe, entering with Silvius, chides Rosalind for revealing the contents of her letter. She replies that she wishes to seem spiteful towards her on purpose and bids Phebe love Silvius who dotes upon her. Phebe bids him tell Ganymede what it is to love.

Silvius, Phebe and Orlando all echo to the refrain of unrequited love, with Rosalind joining in, but in a position to arrange for appropriate requitals on the following day when everybody's desires will be fulfilled.

> The love of Oliver and Celia is the final example in the play of 'love at first sight', amusingly recounted to Orlando by Rosalind. Thereafter she speaks 'in sober meanings' (V.2.66). This sobriety underpins the comically romantic refrains on the nature of love, as Phebe, Orlando and the still disguised Rosalind echo the idealistic definitions and feeling of Silvius and prepares us for the solemnity of the last scene in which the lovers are finally paired off.

11 **estate** settle

28 **I know where you are** I know what you mean

30 **thrasonical** boastful

36 **degrees** steps of the stairs and stages in the process

37 **incontinent** in the first occurrence, immediately, in the second, unchaste

39 **clubs** heavy sticks

51 **of good conceit** of good understanding

58–9 **a magician ... not damnable** a white magician, not one involved in black magic regarded as the work of the devil

60 **as your gesture cries it out** as your behaviour proclaims it

63 **inconvenient** inappropriate

64–5 **human as she is** in the flesh, not a phantom

93 **observance** respect, dutiful service

98 **why blame you me to love you** why do you blame me for loving you

104–5 **the howling of Irish wolves against the moon** wolves were still common in Ireland in Shakespeare's time when it was believed that they howled with greater intensity at the full moon

SCENE 3 Touchstone announces that he and Audrey will be married the next day. Two pages sing them a song

Touchstone affirms to Audrey's great satisfaction that they will be married on the next day. Two of the Duke's pages enter and sing a song 'It was a lover and his lass'.

The projected marriage of Touchstone and Audrey continues the marriage theme and provides the occasion for one of Shakespeare's most well-known songs on the love in springtime. Typically, the romantic note is not unalloyed, succeeded as it is by the unappreciative comments of Touchstone.

4–5 **a woman of the world** a married woman

10 **clap into't roundly** go straight into it directly

hawking clearing the throat noisily

14 **on a horse** on one horse

18 **ring time** the time when lovers exchange rings

21 **Between the acres of the rye** that is, on the unploughed land between the ploughed acre strips

35 **the prime** the spring, figuratively the springtime of human life, youth

40 **matter in the ditty** substance in the words of the song

41 **untunable** discordant; Touchstone is saying that he does not think much of the song. A surprising utterance; 'tunable' seems to be expected

SCENE 4 **With the company assembled next day Rosalind, as Ganymede, secures various promises of marriage from the protagonists. Touchstone arrives with Audrey and engages in humorous banter with Jaques. Rosalind and Celia, now dressed as themselves, enter with a masquer in the role of Hymen who unites the four couples. Jaques de Boys arrives with news of Duke Fredericks's conversion to the religious life and his restoration of the Duke and his followers. The melancholy Jaques decides to follow Duke Frederick's example**

In the presence of the Duke, the still disguised Rosalind confirms the pact she has made. The Duke agrees to give Rosalind in marriage to Orlando and Orlando to take her. Phebe agrees to marry Rosalind if s/he agrees and if not then to marry Silvius who agrees to take her. When Touchstone and Audrey enter, Touchstone engages in an extended witty exchange with Jaques as he introduces him to the Duke. A **masquer** enters with Rosalind and Celia now out of disguise; the masquer as Hymen sings a wedding song. Rosalind seals the bargains made and Hymen pairs off the couples finishing with a wedding hymn. The Duke welcomes his niece and daughter. Phebe accepts Silvius. Jaques de Boys, the second son of Sir Rowland, enters with the news that Duke Frederick, who had approached the forest with a large army with the purpose of capturing Duke Senior and putting him to the sword, on meeting an old religious man at the edge of the forest and having communication with him, has experienced a change of heart and decided to bequeath his crown to his banished brother, to restore lands seized from those he banished and to withdraw from the world. The Duke welcomes the news but decrees that the marriages be completed in the forest with appropriate celebration and revelry before they all return to their former fortunes and status. So impressed with Duke Frederick's conversion is the melancholy Jaques that he decides he will join him. Alone on stage, Rosalind in the epilogue appeals to the audience for their favour and applause. (The interlude between Touchstone and Jaques (lines 35–104) is discussed in Textual Analysis.)

The final comic interchange between Touchstone and Jaques in which Touchstone mocks aspects of courtly life and manners precedes the **denouement**, easily brought about by the revelation of Rosalind's disguise. With the entry of Hymen comes solemnity and ceremony, marked by the formal wedding song. News of the conversion of Duke Frederick prepares the way for the restoration of the old order now made wiser by experience. The decision of Jaques to join the Duke means that he too has made a resolution appropriate to his temperament and character, so that it cannot be said that he is excluded from the play's harmonious and happy ending. There are no loose ends. Rosalind remarks that it is not convention to give the last word (the epilogue) to a lady; but as the central character who is the engineer of Shakespeare's plot it is highly fitting that she speaks it and so brings the play to end on a note of good humour and insinuating comic banter.

5 **compact is urged** agreement is affirmed

32 **desperate** dangerous

35–6 **another flood ... couples ... to the ark** a comic allusion to the Biblical account of Noah's ark to which the animals came two by two

42–3 **put me to my purgation** put me to the test so that I can prove myself

43 **trod a measure** danced a solemn dance

45 **undone three tailors** ruined them by not paying his bills

49 **the seventh cause** the Lie Direct (V.4.93)

53 **God 'ild** God reward

54 **copulatives** couples son to be joined in marriage

55–6 **marriage binds and blood breaks** vows bind but sexual desire leads to adultery

61 **swift and sententious** quick-witted and full of sayings

62 **fool's bolt** alludes to the proverb 'A fool's bolt is soon shot' meaning that a fool utters his opinion too hastily and thus renders further discussion or exploration superfluous; the phrase also has a bawdy meaning referring to premature ejaculation

63 **dulcet diseases** sweet afflictions referring in part to sayings and witticisms but perhaps also alluding to venereal diseases which though not sweet in themselves might be sweet in the catching

73–4 **disabled my judgement** disparaged my opinion

78 **Countercheck** rebuke in reply to one received

Lie Circumstantial a contradiction given indirectly by circumstances

83 **Lie Direct** tell me in no uncertain terms that I was lying

84 **measured swords** in duelling, to ensure that one party did not have a longer sword than the other and so an advantage; here the reference is to verbal sparring

87 **in print** with precision; having consulted printed manuals

by the book formal, according to the rules

97–8 **swore brothers** became sworn brothers

103 **stalking-horse** either a real horse or a decoy under the cover of which a hunter approaches his game. The Duke means that Touchstone's apparent folly is a pretext or disguise that enables him to penetrate the defences of his satirical targets

105 **Hymen** the Roman god of the marriage ceremony, in the form of a young man carrying a torch

107 **Atone together** suggest the atonement, making amendment and making things one, the conclusion to which the whole comedy has been working

138 **Juno's crown** Juno, wife of Jupiter and symbol of female authority, was the Roman goddess who presided over marriage

153 **Addressed a mighty power** prepared a mighty army

154 **In his own conduct** under his personal command

165 **offerest fairly** bring a good gift

170 **shrewd** irksome, harsh

172 **According to the measure of their states** in proportion to their rank

176 **With measure heaped in joy to th'measures fall** with your cup of joy filled to the brim begin the dance

179 **pompous** full of pomp and splendour

181 **convertites** those converted to a religious life

198 **bush** advertisement

203 **insinuate with** work subtly on

205 **conjure** make a solemn appeal

Part three

Critical approaches

Plot and design: comparison with the source

Shakespeare's design and preoccupations in *As You Like It* are most readily illustrated in a comparison of the play with its main source, the popular prose **romance** *Rosalynde or Euphues' Golden Legacy* by Thomas Lodge printed in 1590 and reprinted several times (1592, 1596 and 1598 and subsequently). In an address 'To the Gentleman Reader', Lodge has the phrase 'If you like it, so', perhaps the source of Shakespeare's throw away title *As You Like It*. The narrator, Euphues, promises that his readers will find 'love anatomised by Euphues' and offers a serious tale: 'here is helleborus, bitter in taste but beneficial in trial', with a clear moral: 'Here gentlemen, may you see in Euphues Golden Legacie, that such as neglect their father's precepts, incur much prejudice; that division in nature, as it is a blemish in nurture, so 'tis a breach of good fortunes; that virtue is not measured by birth but by action; that younger brethren, though inferior in years, yet may be superior to honours; that concord be the sweetest conclusion, and amity betwixt brothers more forcible than fortune.' This might equally serve as a moral, not the only one, for Shakespeare's play. What Shakespeare owes to Lodge for the general outline of his plot will be apparent from this summary account of *Rosalynde*.

On his deathbed, Sir John of Bordeaux (Sir Rowland de Boys in Shakespeare) bequeaths the greatest part of his estate to his youngest son Rosader (Orlando). But the eldest son Saladyne (Oliver) does not honour the will and keeps Rosader in subjection. After a time, Rosader, now grown up, asserts himself and the brothers come to blows. When Torismond (Duke Frederick), who has usurped the throne of France from King Gerismond (Duke Senior), holds a wrestling tournament, Saladyne bribes the wrestler to kill Rosader. Inspired by the beauty of Rosalind, the daughter of the exiled Gerismond and companion of Alinda (Celia) daughter of the usurper Torismond, Rosader kills the wrestler. Impressed by his good looks and valour, Rosalind falls in love with Rosader and sends him a jewel from her neck; he replies by sending her a love poem that he has composed in courtly style.

Fearful that Rosalind will marry and that her husband will seize the throne in her right, Torismond banishes Rosalind from the court suggesting that she seek her father who is now living the life of an outlaw in the Forest of Arden. Alinda makes an impassioned plea on Rosalind's behalf to no avail. She decides to accompany Rosalind into exile. They go disguised as Ganymede and Aliena into the forest. After a journey of three days, they come upon the plaintive verses on a tree in the forest of the shepherd Montanus (Silvius) who has been rejected by the hard-hearted shepherdess Phebe, then overhear the young Montanus and aged Corydon (Corin) discoursing poetically on the plight of the rejected Montanus. Aliena introduces herself and Ganymede to the shepherds. After Corydon has praised the life of the country which is not affected by envy or ambition, Aliena bids Corydon send for his landlord so that she can buy his farm and flocks and live a **pastoral** life of quiet contentment in the forest.

Meanwhile Saladyne has enlisted the support of the sheriff and his men against Rosader who together with his old servant Adam Spencer wards off the sheriff and escapes to the Forest of Arden. After a six day journey, they are enfeebled through lack of food. Rosader comes upon Gerismond celebrating his birthday with venison and wine. He challenges him to give him food. After he has returned bearing Adam on his shoulders, he is applauded for fulfilling the offices of a true friend.

The melancholy Rosader encounters Ganymede and Aliena in the forest. Aliena suggests to Rosalind that they have some sport with him so as Ganymede she questions him about his love for Rosalind and elicits love poems from him. Ganymede then asks Rosader to let her see how he can woo, saying she will take the part of Rosalind. They sing a love duet in which Rosalind first plays hard to get then yields to the persuasions of Rosader. Aliena then offers to play the priest so that they can have a marriage: 'and so with a smile and a blush, they made up this jesting match, that after proved to be a marriage in earnest, Rosader full little thinking he had wooed and won his Rosalind'.

Meanwhile Saladyne, banished by Torismond and having wandered into the forest, falls asleep in a cave and is spotted by a hungry lion who waits to see if he will move 'for lions hate to prey upon dead carcasses'. Rosader comes by, recognises his sleeping brother and has a long debate as to whether to save him. Eventually he decides to kill the lion and is wounded in the process. Saladyne does not recognise his brother but confesses his guilt and shame at his treatment of Rosader to whom he desires to make amends. Rosader reveals himself and the brothers are reconciled.

Aliena and Ganymede are set upon by a band of rascally outlaws. Rosader is outnumbered and unable to save them. Saladyne comes to the rescue. Aliena thanks him and they begin to fall in love. She and Ganymede overhear the love suit of Montanus being rejected by Phebe. Ganymede intervenes to rebuke Phebe who falls in love with the supposed youth. Saladyne courts Aliena. Phebe, sickened by her new found love, sends Montanus to Ganymede with a letter pleading her cause. Montanus begs Ganymede to take pity on Phebe, proving his loyalty and putting Phebe's happiness before his own. Ganymede elicits a promise from Phebe that if she ceases to be enamoured of him, she will then turn her attentions to Montanus.

Preparations are made for the marriage of Aliena and Saladyne. Gerismond hears Montanus's love poetry addressed to Phebe, and questions her. Phebe says she is in love with Ganymede and reveals their previous bargain. Ganymede offers to provide a solutions by magic; she then dresses in women's attire and reveals herself. The three marriages are celebrated. Fernandine, the second son of Sir Richard, enters with news that Torismond has come with an armed force to the edge of the forest. Gerismond, Rosader and Saladyne arm and engage him in battle where he is defeated and killed. They all return to Paris and resume their former lives.

Shakespeare has followed the plot of Lodge surprisingly closely or, put another way, it is perhaps surprising to find that so many elements of the play come directly from the original **romance**. Here the love element is central, with the disguise providing the principal intrigue. The various courtships are conducted in a very traditional chivalric style with the lovers writing poems to their loved ones. Needless to say the protagonists all conform to typical notions of beauty and goodness. There is the simple opposition between good and evil with the hero being tested and proving his worth in an initial trial of strength and then subsequently showing constancy to his beloved and other moral qualities. The encounter with the lion is a typical romance motif. Shakespeare has retained too the

French connection of this particular generic mode which had originated in France; in the names of two of the characters, Le Beau and Amiens, in a number of French words and in the location of Arden itself which suggests the Ardennes as well as the forest of Arden in Warwickshire. Members of the Elizabethan audience, whether or not they knew the specific source, must have recognised the affinities of *As You Like It* with a **genre** that was more familiar to them than it is to us and have attuned their expectations accordingly.

Many elements of the original romance as well as the outline of its story are retained but the dramatisation of it which resulted in a romantic comedy involved many changes and additions. The long prose romance is naturally greatly condensed and the time scale compressed. The play starts in the middle of things with Orlando's self assertion and not with the will of Sir Rowland or the usurpation of Duke Senior which we hear about in a recapitulation. Shakespeare starts with and concentrates upon Orlando rather than on Duke Senior who does not appear until the second act because his chosen emphasis is upon love. In the play, the two Dukes, like Oliver and Orlando, are brothers whereas Torismond and Gerismond are not related. The theme of brother against brother is thus intensified in this symmetrical arrangement. There is further symmetry in the parallel conversions of Oliver and Duke Frederick. The suddenness of these conversions which are not made to be realistic might even be regarded as feature typical of romance. In the source the evil ruler is killed whereas in *As You Like It* there are no deaths (Orlando manages to defeat Charles without killing him). Although the potential for evil is there, Shakespeare's play turns out to be even more benign than the romance which is its source.

Rosalynde is not only a **romance** but a specific kind of romance popular in late Elizabethan England, a **pastoral romance**. Most of it is set in the countryside; Corydon, Montanus and Phebe are joined in their idealised **pastoral** life as shepherds by Ganymede and Aliena. When Aliena meets Corydon in the forest, she sees the life of the country in ideal terms: 'I wander in this forest to light upon some cottage where I and my page may dwell: for I mean to buy some farm, and a flock of sheep, and so become a shepherdess, meaning to live low [humbly], and content me with a country life; for I have heard the swains say, that they drunk without suspicion and slept without care.' Corydon, in words that

Shakespeare probably had in mind when he composed the Duke's praise of life in the forest in contrast to 'the envious court' (II.1.4) confirms her view: 'Envy stirs not us, we covet not to climbe, our desires mount not above our fortunes. Care [worry, stress] cannot harbour in our cottages not do our homely couches know broken slumbers: as we exceed not in diet, so we have enough to satisfy: and, mistress, I have so much Latin, *satis est quod sufficit*' [what satisfies is enough]. How many Elizabethan shepherds had even a smattering of the learned language? This is rural life as seen from the standpoint of an educated man like Lodge who was fully conversant with the life of the courtier.

A pastoral romance is not so called simply because it is set in the countryside and may seem to value the simple life of the country above that of the court where everybody is jockeying for position, social climbing and back-stabbing. *Rosalynde* contains thematic and stylistic elements that allude to the specific literary tradition that we call pastoral. All the poetic wooing including that between Rosalind and Rosader is in the pastoral mode, cast in the form of Eclogues and songs that recall the love songs of the writers of classical pastoral, Theocritus and Virgil. In these poets the shepherds sing in a mellifluous style of their trials and triumphs in love; they are, in fact not realistic shepherds who have to work hard for a living and deal with the more unsavoury aspects of animal husbandry but budding poets in shepherdly disguise who can spend their time romantically mooning about love. The plot of *As You Like It* retains these pastoral characters (Corin, Silvius and Phebe) their mode of wooing and some of the pastoral conventions with which they and the literary world they inhabit are associated. For instance, at the beginning of the play, the wrestler Charles reports that the Duke is in the Forest of Arden living like 'the old Robin Hood of England': 'they say many young gentlemen flock to him every day, and fleet the time carelessly as they did in the golden world' (I.1.111). This is a literary allusion to the classical idea of the golden age of innocence and peace when men lived in harmony with themselves and nature, in an eternal springtime, while nature poured forth her gifts unbidden without the necessity of the plough, an cluster of ideas that came to be associated with the pastoral ideal.

As a pastoral romance, *Rosalynde* is a serious work. It is not wholly without moments of humour but any humour is entirely incidental. The comedy of *As You Like It*, however, embraces not only the principals as they fall in love but also extends to the pastoral characters; in his debate with Touchstone on the respective merits of country life, Corin proves to be a more down-to-earth shepherd than Corydon when he talks amongst other unsavoury things of the greasiness of his sheep (III.2.51) and Touchstone reminds us, humorously, that Corin makes his living out 'the copulation of cattle' (III.2.76). Corin is therefore a fairly realistic shepherd and implicitly undercuts his literary forbears. Silvius and Phebe and their mode of expression are much more explicitly mocked in the play. When Corin invites Rosalind and Celia to witness 'a pageant truly played, / Between the pale complexion of true love / And the red glow of scorn and proud disdain' (III.4.47) he is introducing a stock situation familiar to his audience which is played out in terms that are not wholly serious. These are clichéd characters who speak and act in extravagant terms that are mocked by Rosalind. Furthermore, the presence of realistic country characters like the 'ill-favoured' Audrey, who does not understand the meaning of the word poetical (III.3.15) and therefore is hardly an idealised shepherdess and William the country bumpkin serve to throw the unreality of the pastoral figures into sharp relief. They and their conventional style become a source of humour as they are not in Lodge.

A further perspective upon the pastoral and courtly wooing is suggested in the simplicity of the songs in the play. With the exception of the wedding hymn at the end, these are not written in the high style to which the courting characters aspire (sometimes with comic effect) but have affinities with a simpler folk tradition. The songs are more realistic than literary pastoral evoking the world that we experience of seasonal change that includes the harshness of winter and rough winds. Against this simple realism the artificiality of pastoral conventions and imagery can be seen for what they are.

There are other changes that may be considered under the heading of characterisation which serve to create the comedy and enhance the critical perspective with which the pastoral romance is viewed. In the first place there are additional characters, fully integrated into the main design rather than being kept more or less separate in a parallel sub-plot, who allow a different undercutting perspective on the **genre** of romance.

THE FOOL

Touchstone, the fool, is an earthy and unruly incarnation of the comic spirit for whom there is no equivalent in Lodge. Although he is referred to as a clown in the cast list and a 'natural' by Rosalind when he first appears (I.2.47) that is, an idiot, he is a wise fool (and in fact a very learned fool), a character type who appears in other Shakespeare plays (for example, the fool Feste in *Twelfth Night* (1599) and the fool in *King Lear* (1605). His prototype is the court jester, a licensed clown, whose mask of folly allows him in the course of his clowning to utter truths that might be unconventional or daring. It is significant that it is Rosalind who suggests that he shall accompany herself and Celia into the forest. The **wit** she displays is akin to his. He is not named until the stage direction at the head of Act II Scene 4 (discussed in Textual Analysis) which has led to speculation that he was also in disguise in the forest, not now a popular view. It has been suggested that when he created the part Shakespeare had a particular actor in mind, Robert Armin.

Whether or not this is so, his part is fully integrated into the action and therefore more closely implicated in its central themes than other Shakespearean fools in the plays in which they occur. He is not only witty at the expense of the lovers but himself becomes one of the four pairs of lovers through his marriage to Audrey. His presence accompanying Rosalind in so many of the scenes, his parody of Orlando's sentimental verse and his ungallant wooing of Audrey sustains the wit of the comedy and offers an unromantic perspective on the theme of love which is at the play's centre. He is a sensualist who is marrying for sex and therefore offers a very earthy view of the basis of marriage. This earthiness is reflected in his language in which there are many bawdy double meanings. At the same time his fooling is not all on these lines. His debate with Corin on the merits of country life, however absurdly argued in its parts, does raise one of the central issues of the play and offers a corrective to sentimental or over idealised views of life in the forest as well as raising an issue that recurs intermittently: the proper use of time. He is similarly undeceived about life at court and is the cause of much humour at the expense of the superficiality of courtly manners particularly in the final scene where his method and wit are appreciated by Duke

Senior (see Textual Analysis). His name suggests something about his role in the play; he is a touchstone whose mask of folly serves to try and test the value of things in the course of which he exposes the affectation and folly of others.

Jaques

Although he is not a comic figure, the melancholy Jaques, a character who is a Shakespearean addition who has no equivalent in Lodge, has a caustic **wit** and a grumbling **malcontented** perspective that equally undercuts the spirit of **romance**.

He is what might be called a 'humour character', that is, his character and behaviour represents a particular psychological disposition or type, in his case, the melancholy man: Orlando calls him Monsieur Melancholy (III.2.286). This does not simply mean that he is sad but that he suffers from an excess of the black bile (one of the four medieval humours which constitute the human being) which gives him a rather jaundiced view upon life (it is often said that he has a cynical view of human nature) resulting in a disposition to satire and invective. When he articulates his wish to 'Cleanse the foul body of th'infected world' (II.7.60), the Duke attributes this desire to his own previous licentiousness that has turned sour. There is no other reference to this in the play and Jaques instead of defending himself offers a general defence of his satirical tendency (II.7.70). In fact he tells us little about himself. When he later talks to Rosalind about his melancholy of which he seems rather too consciously proud, he associates it with contemplation of his travels 'in which my often rumination wraps me in a most humorous sadness' (IV.1.18). Rosalind merrily takes this to mean that he is sad because he has sold his lands 'to see other men's' (IV.1.21) to little effect. She makes a joke of it but Jaques does not tell us any more and remains something of a mystery.

He is chiefly associated with two parts of the play. First there is the extravagant picture of him given by one of the Duke's lords lamenting and moralising upon the fate of the wounded deer which becomes not only an occasion for his satire upon mankind but also the cause of the Duke's pleasure at the spectacle (II.1.26). Secondly there is the famous speech about the seven ages of man 'All the world's a stage, / And all the men and women merely players' (II.7.140–1). This offers a gloomy view in which mankind is seen to play a series of prescribed parts. At the conclusion Orlando enters bearing the aged Adam on his shoulders. Neither character entirely fits the stereotype of the speech; Orlando is more than 'the lover, / Sighing like a furnace, with a woeful ballad / Made to his mistress' eyebrow' (II.7.148–50) and Adam, eighty years old is physically infirm but mentally alert. Their mutual loyalty demonstrates a human dimension that puts a perspective upon the speech. Jaques's perspective therefore is a limited one and only one of many in the play so that he is not, as has sometimes been said, the voice and spokesman of Shakespeare himself.

Despite the fact that as a melancholy character in a comedy he is out of place, he is not seriously ridiculed or punished for his 'humour'. He takes little part in the action; one of his main functions is to sound a jarring discordant note (the Duke says he is 'compact of jars' (II.7.5) which diversifies the tonal range of the play. His alternative point of view is reflected in his ascetic rejection of love and marriage at the end in favour of a religious life and in his a conscious refusal to join in the happy harmony 'So to your pleasures: / I am for other than for dancing measures' (V.4.189–90). In fact he is almost allowed the last word before Rosalind's epilogue. (For further comment on Jaques see Textual Analysis.)

ROSALIND

Shakespeare's Rosalind is a much more dynamic, attractive and three dimensional character than the conventional romantic heroine. Lodge's *Rosalynde*, of course, is not a *comic* **romance**. Here we come to the nub of the difference between the play and its source and to the crux of Shakespeare's design in *As You Like It*. She is not only the central character but also through her witty inventiveness in manipulating her disguise a prime source of the comedy; and she becomes much more dominant in the play than in the romance despite the fact that the latter takes its name from her. Shakespeare has endowed Rosalind with a quick-witted verbal intelligence. In combats of wit she outshines Orlando and can hold her own with Touchstone and Jaques. She is loquacious and eloquent with much to say and has by far the largest part.

At court, as the daughter of the ruling Duke, Celia has a superior status and social power that is reflected in her role in both the romance and the play where she has the first word in bidding Rosalind be merry. But the primacy of Rosalind as the agent of Shakespeare's comedy is immediately apparent in her reply to Celia: 'From henceforth I will, coz, and devise sports. Let me see – what think you of falling in love?' (I.2.23–4). Although Celia suggests that they should disguise themselves, it is Rosalind's idea to take upon herself the disguise of a man. Once she has donned her doublet and hose she becomes much more dominant in playing the masculine role; in the forest, she takes the initiative in both practical matters in buying the farm (initiated by Aliena in Lodge) and in the devising of the sports that constitute the comedy, for example, in organising the mock marriage (done by Aliena in Lodge). In Lodge, Rosalynde does not use her disguise to reveal to her lover and the audience the absurdity of conventional wooing and expose the unreality of it posturing style. Instead she joins in, using the same language and style as Phebe. Nor is it so clear in Lodge that she is testing Orlando and the motif of the love-cure, initiated by Rosalind both to tease and to educate Orlando, is a Shakespearean importation. She is much more determined, too, in her serious intervention in the love affair between Silvius and Phebe; she fulfils her own intention: 'I will prove a busy actor in their play' (III.4.55). Her business makes her the chief engineer of the plot and its outcome.

She sustains her principal role as the main engineer of the plot by virtue of strength of character, self knowledge and a disposition that is sportive and playful. Even at court where she is oppressed by her situation, when cajoled by Celia she cheers up and engages in humorous banter with Touchstone and Le Beau. When banished by Duke Frederick, she is dignified in her denials showing an underlying moral strength. When she has fallen in love in true romantic fashion at first sight with Orlando, she is frank about the physical nature of her attraction. To Celia's early question as to whether her melancholy is all for her father she replies, in a line that has sometimes been suppressed in more prudish productions, 'No, some of it is for my child's father' (I.3.11). Once in the forest, disguised as Ganymede her strength is put to the test; she is wittily conscious of her new role: 'I could find it in my heart to disgrace my man's apparel, and to cry like a woman, but I must comfort the weaker vessel, as doublet-and-hose ought to show itself courageous to petticoat' (II.4.4–7) She is again wittily conscious about her disguise when Celia's is slow to reveal the identity of the author of the verses they have found on the trees: 'Dost thou think because I am caparisoned like a man, I have doublet and hose in my disposition?' (III.2.188–90). She sustains the disguise with panache, making rude jokes about cuckoldry with Jaques for example, lapsing only when she faints upon hearing of Orlando's wound.

In fact in the matter of the disguise, she makes a virtue of necessity. She becomes in her own words 'a saucy lackey' (III.2.287) in her treatment of Orlando and makes the most of her disguise to elicit expressions of love from him and to ridicule the typical posture of the sentimental lover, captured in Jaques's speech on the seven ages and played out by Orlando when he goes around the forest pinning up verses to his Rosalind on trees. Her denial that he is a true lover because she cannot recognise in him all the conventional signs of the love-sickness (III.2.358) brings to bear a perspective of witty realism upon the foolish postures of love. This realism is again apparent in her dismissal of Orlando's extravagant claim that he is dying of love (IV.1.84) and in her final impatience after the romantic litany of love between herself, Orlando, Silvius and Phebe which she declares to be 'like the howling of Irish wolves against the moon' (V.2.104–5). In the 'love cure', she wittily exploits conventional ideas about the changeability of women (III.2.392) to test Orlando's romantic feelings and to educate him in the ways of the world (IV.1.135). In being honest about her own feelings and manipulating those of Orlando, Phebe and Silvius, all being conducted in a spirit of witty realism, she shows us much more effectively than Lodge what he had promised in *Rosalynde*: 'love anatomised'.

CELIA

Celia fulfils the role of the true friend throughout the play. As the daughter of the ruling Duke, she is in a position of power until the restoration of Duke Senior at the end, but she never seeks to assert any advantage over her cousin. On the contrary she is clearly embarrassed by the conduct of her father which she does not seek to excuse. She goes out of her way to be generous to Rosalind saying that when he dies she will make Rosalind his heir (I.2.17). The relationship between the cousins is very credibly presented. They have much in common; Celia, in fact can be said to be a more moderate version of Rosalind. She is witty and playful in her own right and is not simply a 'feed' for Rosalind's superior wit. At court, in conversation with Touchstone and Le Beau both women engage in humorous banter more or less equally. Once in the forest, Rosalind is the dominant figure, but Celia often teases Rosalind playfully suggesting that Orlando is not in love (III.4.19). In fact Rosalind in love with Orlando has to endure from Celia the kind of good-natured satirical teasing that she herself inflicts upon others. Rosalind gets a taste of her own medicine from Celia and through her detached eyes we see that Rosalind is not exempt from the folly of love. Yet even here they prove to be more or less equal; Rosalind comically describing Celia's whirlwind romance with Oliver (V.2.28) is able to have the last laugh. In Lodge's *Rosalynde*, Oliver first rescues the women from an attack by outlaws so that she is in his debt and therefore well disposed to him. Without this motivation in Shakespeare, her instant falling in love seems more comically abrupt.

Orlando

Orlando, the victim of injustice at the hands of his elder brother, has all that it takes to be a romantic hero. His self-assertion, now that he has grown up, is the initiating factor which sets the plot in motion. He is a spirited youth, the son of a revered father, who tells his brother Oliver to his face, 'The spirit of my father grows strong in me and I will no longer endure it' (I.1.65–6) He has physical strength and courage; he is not afraid to come to blows with his brother and despite his youth and against the expectation of Duke Frederick, Rosalind and Celia who try to dissuade him from what they regard as an unequal contest he achieves a heroic victory over the wrestler Charles. In the forest, he shows courage in demanding food from the Duke and later in his killing of the lioness. This latter is evidence too of a kind of moral courage when he forgives his wicked brother Oliver. His goodness is also apparent in his considerate treatment of his servant the aged and enfeebled Adam.

His courage is apparent too in his verbal defiance of his brother. He shows not only defiance but superior wit and gets the better of him in argument. In an exchange with Jaques, who has to admit that he is 'full of pretty answers' (III.2.263) he similarly comes out on top, giving as good as he gets. His plea to the Duke beginning 'Speak you so gently?' (II.7.107) is lyrically eloquent and moving: 'Let gentleness my strong enforcement be' (II.7.119).

Despite the lack of schooling of which he complains at the beginning, he is, in the words of Oliver, 'gentle, never schooled yet learned, full of noble device' (I.1.155–6). The meaning of 'gentle' is primarily to do with gentility rather than gentleness in the modern sense. It is his innate gentility that guides him in his moral choice when he later spares his brother. He is therefore a worthy suitor of Rosalind with whom he falls romantically in love at first sight.

As a lover, his role in the play is to be the embodiment of the typical courtly wooer; as such, he pens verses (not very good ones, full of conventional images and exaggerated expressions) and pins them onto trees. He talks about loving for ever and of dying for love. His motive in agreeing to Ganymede's suggestion of mock-wooing is that this gives him an opportunity to 'be talking of her' (IV.1.82). When eventually he tells her that he 'can live no longer by thinking' (V.2.48), Rosalind then reveals her proposal to bring his love to him by magic.

THEMES

ROMANTIC LOVE

The harmonious ending which celebrates the marriages of Rosalind and Orlando, Celia and Oliver and Phebe and Silvius upholds the values of romantic love as they are to be found in Shakespeare's source (Thomas Lodge, *Rosalynde or Euphues' Golden Legacy*) as described above (see Structure). Yet through the use of the disguise many features of **romance** are mocked and ridiculed. The postures of the courtly wooer are mocked when Orlando's verses addressed to Rosalind become the occasion of satire. The disguised Rosalind mocks the affectations of the courtly lover when she tells Orlando that he is too smartly dressed and controlled in his demeanour to be taken seriously as a man in love (Act III Scene 2).. Rosalind's 'cure' for love-madness is to present Orlando with a most unflattering picture of women (III.2.391–9) that pours cold water on his romantic enthusiasm. Although he rejects the cure, a note of realism is introduced which is further reinforced when, in response to his avowal of eternal love, she bids him:

> Say 'a day' without the 'ever'. No, no, Orlando, men are April when they woo, December when they wed; maids are May when they are maids, but the sky changes when they are wives. (IV.1.135–8)

When he expresses the opinion that if rejected he will die (IV.1.84) this extravagant attitude is again mocked and shown to be an illusion. Alongside this is mockery of the old-style **pastoral** love represented by Phebe and Silvius. Like Orlando, Phebe is schooled by Rosalind to accept realities in relation to love.

In stark opposition to the theme of romantic love is its very unromantic opposite in the relationship between Touchstone, who is marrying for sex and Audrey who simply wishes to become a woman of the world (V.3.4) that is, a respectable married woman. Here the mockery of romance which is a general feature of the play as a whole (and reflected in the many bawdy undertones) is most obviously felt.

Yet despite the mockery, Rosalind's love for Orlando is genuine and sincere. She proclaims it ecstatically to Celia and we believe her:

> O coz, coz, coz, my pretty little coz, that thou didst know how many fathom deep I am in love! But it cannot be sounded: my affection hath an unknown bottom, like the Bay of Portugal. (IV.1.190–3)

The play therefore endorses the notion of romantic love but without illusions.

It may also be said that built into the structure of *As You Like It* is a critique of the basic assumptions of the romantic **genre** upon which it depends, but this critique does not destroy the illusion. On the contrary it helps to sustain it by offering alternatives, even that of Jaques who is not of the marrying kind. These alternative perspectives serve to embrace and channel the audience's scepticism so that the ending can be enjoyed by the romantic and the unromantic, and by the idealistic and the cynical alike, who can take the play and its romantic theme 'as they like it'.

LOVE AS FOLLY

Love involves all its devotees, whether romantic or not, in folly. The pervading presence of the fool, Touchstone, brings folly in its train and he is not only present as a commentator on the love affairs of the principals but is himself one of the lovers in the play. His own admission of his foolish behaviour as a lover 'We that are true lovers run into strange capers' (II.4.49–50) echoes the earlier words of the most romantic lover, Silvius, when he says to the aged Corin:

> If thou rememberest not the slightest folly
> That ever love did make thee run into,
> Thou hast not loved. (II.4.30–2)

His sententious remark 'but as all is mortal in nature, so is all nature in love mortal [abundant] in folly' (II.4.50–1) might be regarded as stating one of the play's main themes.

The plot involves all the lovers in some kind of folly. Phebe, falling in love with the disguised Rosalind, looks foolish and behaves foolishly throughout. Folly is exposed in Orlando but also in the excitable Rosalind who becomes the victim of the sensible Celia's teasing **wit** (Act III Scene 4). Celia herself is made to look slightly foolish in the rapid account of her headlong descent into love for Oliver (V.2.29). Although it is a joke and a game, the motif of the love-cure promotes the idea that love is akin to madness. What Theseus says of lovers and madmen in Shakespeare's earlier comedy *A Midsummer Night's Dream* might equally well be prompted by the action of *As You Like It*:

> Lovers and madmen have such seething brains,
> Such shaping fantasies, that apprehend
> More than cool reason ever comprehends.
> The lunatic, the lover, and the poet
> Are of imagination all compact. (V.1.4–8)

THE COUNTRY VERSUS THE COURT

This is a central opposition in the play and raises one of its central themes. Life at the court of the tyrannical Frederick is corrupt, dangerous and restricting. Life in the Forest of Arden is simple and free. As they are about to depart for the forest, Celia remarks, 'Now go in we content / To liberty, and not to banishment' (I.3.135–6). To a certain extent life in the forest is idealised. The wrestler Charles does much to create this mood when he tells Oliver of the condition of Duke Senior:

> They say he is already in the Forest of Arden, and many merry men with him; and there they live like the old Robin Hood of England: they say many young gentlemen flock to him every day, and fleet the time carelessly as they did in the golden world. (I.1.108–12)

The Duke's celebrated speech at the opening of Act II when the scene shifts to the forest for the first time draws an explicit contrast between life in the forest and 'the painted pomp' of 'the envious court' (II.1.4). Yet the picture he paints contains its own hardship. He feels winter's cold and the harshness of the elements; this is reality in contrast to the flattery he had known at court. Nevertheless the speech ends on an ideal note as the Duke 'Finds tongues in trees, books in the running brooks, / Sermons in stones, and good in everything' (II.1.16–17). Later there is praise of the natural life away from the world of ambition in the song 'Under the greenwood tree' (II.5.1).

Immediately after the Duke's speech comes the equally famous account of Jaques's lament for the sobbing deer in which he accuses the Duke and his followers of being usurpers in the forest (II.1.27). Jaques too produces a parody of 'Under the greenwood tree' in which he mocks the folly of anyone who leaves 'his wealth and ease, / A stubborn will to please' (II.5.49–50). Touchstone is not happy in the forest, remarking, 'When I was at home, I was in a better place' (II.4.14). He conducts a debate with Corin, a realistic shepherd who feels the effects of a bad landlord (II.4.77), comparing the merits of a shepherd's life with the life that he has come from: 'In respect that it is solitary, I like it very well; but in respect that it is private it is a very vile life. Now in respect it is in the fields, it pleaseth me well; but in respect it is not in court, it is tedious' (III.2.15–17). He does not altogether get the better of the old shepherd in this wit-combat but amid the absurdity Shakespeare does allow him to make some telling points. (Later, of course, he is equally critical of various aspects of court life.)

More than one perspective is therefore presented upon the life of the forest in the course of the play; there is no black and white contrast. Hence it does not come as a great surprise that at the end of the play, in spite of their avowal never to leave the forest, Duke Senior and his followers immediately return to the court when the opportunity is offered to them. Nevertheless, given the ridiculing of courtly wooing and the movement of the play to something more natural and less affected than traditional modes of feeling and their expression, the balance is weighted in favour of the freer and more natural life that is celebrated in the simple language of the various songs. The setting of the Forest of Arden certainly offers an indirect critique of the supposedly more civilised life of the court.

LANGUAGE

The play's variety is reflected in its language, in the division between prose and verse and in the different kinds of verse. There is the formal poetic eloquence of the speeches of Duke Senior (for example, his opening speech at the beginning of the second act) and of Jaques's disquisition on the seven ages of man (II.7.140ff); the lyrical poetic beauty of Orlando's plea to the Duke for food (II.7.107); the lyrical set piece quintet with its refrain on the subject of what it is to love (V.2.78ff); the extravagant love language of Silvius (e.g. II.5.1ff) and of Orlando's verses to Rosalind (e.g. III.2.121ff) and Phebe's verses to Ganymede (IV.3.41ff); the sweet and affecting simplicity of the various country songs with their folk associations; the dignified formality of Hymen's singing at the end (V.4.105ff); a comic song with its joke about horns (IV.2.10ff); the parodies of Orlando by Touchstone (III.2.97ff) and of 'Under the greenwood tree' by Jaques (II.5.47ff).

The prose of the play, which amounts to more than half of the whole, is characterised by a neat and witty style with a marked use of **wordplay** and **antithesis** whether or not it is humorous. In the second sentence some of the main characteristics of its witty style are already apparent:

> My brother Jaques he *keeps at school*, and report speaks
> *goldenly* of his profit: for my part, *he keeps me rustically*

> *at home*, or, to speak more properly, *stays* me here *at home unkept* – for call you that *'keeping'* for a gentleman of my birth, that differs not from the *stalling* of an ox? (I.1.4–10 – emphasis added)

There is nothing humorous about this opening speech of Orlando on his ill treatment at the hands of his brother but it has a number of wordplays and antitheses that lift it beyond the commonplace and make its message forceful and memorable. The main wordplay, which no attentive listener or reader can miss because Orlando emphatically draws attention to it, turns on two meanings of the word *kept*: 'maintains' and 'restrains' or 'detains', *stays* in Orlando's own explanation. There is a subsidiary play in *stalling* which besides the obvious meaning of 'stabling' also can mean 'impeding' or 'delaying', thus reinforcing *stays*. Commentators also draw attention to a possible play on *goldenly* (gold) and *rustically* (rust). The whole sentence contrasts Oliver's treatment of the two brothers; this contrast is brought out in the arrangement of the opening clauses with its antithesis between the keeping *at school* and the keeping *at home*. Orlando's point is hammered home at the end with the sharp antithesis between 'keeping' for a gentleman' and 'stalling of an ox'. Despite the sophistication of the style with its concentration of effects, the sentence in no way seems precious or mannered; on the contrary, every word contributes to the emphatic rendering of Orlando's physical and emotional situation which is communicated with great clarity.

The wordplay is also a cause of repartee between characters which again may not always be for humorous effect. In the opening angry exchange between Orlando and Oliver there is much verbal sparring including a notable pun. When Orlando seizes his brother by the throat, Oliver exclaims 'Wilt thou lay hands on me, villain?' (I.1.52) Here villain means what it means today, 'rogue', 'evildoer'. Orlando's reply picks up on the root meaning of the word which in the feudal world of the middle ages meant an ordinary villager, a person of ignoble birth. 'I am no villain: I am the younger son of Sir Rowland de Boys; he was my father, and he is thrice a villain that says such a father begot villains'.

Most of the wordplay is for comic effect, though the comic effect may not be the whole point, as in this early exchange between Celia and

Touchstone. Celia has warned the fool not to speak more of matters at court concerning her father:

> TOUCHSTONE: The more pity that *fools* may not speak *wisely* what *wise* men do *foolishly*.
>
> CELIA: By my troth, thou sayest true: for since the *little wit* that fools have was *silenced*, the *little foolery* that *wise* men have makes a *great* show. (I.2.82–6 – emphasis added)

Both speakers make a play on the antithesis between folly and wisdom, but Celia caps what Touchstone says by the addition of two further plays in the antithesis between little **wit** (understanding, wisdom) being extinguished and the great show made by the folly of the wise. The point she makes is delivered with a witty panache but is not said simply for comic effect for it is making a serious comment on the current state of affairs at court; it is nevertheless very pleasing to the mind because of the witty precision of the linguistic arrangement.

This antithetical mode is also very suitable for bringing various oppositions, for example that between town and country, sharply to the fore. This debate is cleverly conducted not only between Corin and Touchstone (III.2.11ff) but also within Touchstone's mind as he weighs the pros and cons. The antithetical mode is taken to absurdity in this instance.

The language of the play is subject to a more complicated patterning than can be achieved by the simple use of antitheses as will be apparent in Rosalind's mocking dismissal of Orlando for lacking the marks of a true lover.

> A lean cheek, which you have not; a blue eye and sunken, which you have not; an unquestionable spirit, which you have not; a beard neglected, which you have not – but I pardon you for that, for simply your having in beard is a younger man's revenue. Then your hose should be ungartered, your bonnet unbanded, your sleeve unbuttoned, your shoe untied, and everything about you demonstrating a careless desolation. But you are no such man: you are rather point-device in

your accoutrements, as loving yourself, than seeming
the lover of any other. (III.2.358–68)

Rosalind's list mocks the conventional attributes of the love-sick courtier, eyes dark with sleeplessness, a spirit not wishing to be questioned and so on. There is some sting in her parenthetical remark that as a youth Orlando has not much beard just as a younger brother has not much money. While his dress should show signs of his distraught state, he is dressed with fastidious precision. This is an exuberant speech that uses the freedom of prose to move with great rapidity and apparent informality. But its great emphasis is nevertheless the product of a skilful rhetorical patterning. The opening has a series of four strong antitheses made emphatic by repetition of the negative statement – 'you have not'. The position of the adjectives is interestingly varied with the second and fourth ('sunken' and 'neglected') coming after the noun. The pattern is interrupted by the humorous jibe about the beard. Then follows another series of four requirements that are not met, in a list that is made emphatically concise by avoidance of unnecessary repetition of the verb 'should be' and by insistent repetition of the negative form of the adjectives which are given extra emphasis by position and extra point in the carefully chosen negative form of the adjective 'careless' in the final phrase. The next short sentence makes its point directly. The final sentence rounds off the whole exercise by offering in its totality a strong **antithesis** to what has preceded it, and containing within itself a second antithesis at the end. The **syntactical** patterning is underscored by repetition of sounds, and by **alliteration** and **assonance**. The patterning is not such that it seems mannered, and there is enough variation and interruption for the illusion of spontaneity but however it might be described it is definitely there. Rosalind makes further effective use of listing and strong antitheses in the speech in which she defines women's changeability and offers to cure Orlando (III.2.389ff).

In the utterances of Touchstone Shakespeare's playing with words is at its most extreme. The fool is a master of a number of witty word games reducing things to absurdity. An early example is his argument about honour prompted by Rosalind's question 'Where learned you that oath' after his use of the courtly cliché 'by mine honour' (I.2.58–60).

> TOUCHSTONE: Of a certain knight that swore by his honour they were good pancakes and swore by his honour the mustard was naught: now I'll stand to it the pancakes were naught and the mustard was good, and yet the knight was not forsworn.
>
> CELIA: How prove you that, in the great heap of your knowledge?
>
> ROSALIND: Ay, marry, now unmuzzle your wisdom.
>
> TOUCHSTONE: Stand you both forth now: stroke your chins and swear by your beards that I am a knave.
>
> CELIA: By our beards – if we had them – thou art.
>
> TOUCHSTONE: By my knavery – if I had it – then I were; but if you swear by that that is not, you are not forsworn: no more was this knight, swearing by his honour, for he never had any; or if he had, he had sworn it away before ever he saw those pancakes or that mustard. (I.2.61–76)

Although commentators suspect that there may be an as yet undiscovered allusion in the joke about mustard and pancakes, the main point of the exchange is clear enough and its humour can still be felt. Touchstone is fooling with words and emptying them of meaning by the inappropriate application of logical argument. The playfulness is enhanced by the neatness of his phrasing and by the increasing precision of the argumentation at the end. 'By my knavery, if I had it, then I were': this further devalues the meaninglessness of the oath upon honour. Both the proof and the expression are clever; Celia and Rosalind rightly acknowledge his knowledge and wisdom. The introduction of this exchange is gratuitous and it is there principally for its own sake to entertain but in the remarks that follow is the clear implication from Touchstone that the court of Frederick is not honourable. But any social comment is rather oblique; the main impression created by this display of cleverness on the part of the wise fool is that words are unreliable ciphers in relation to things and can be as easily twisted into nonsense as they can be used to create meaning.

The effect of the **wordplay** in general is not only highly entertaining and a chief source of humour, it is often subversive in the way it breaks down simple meaning and makes us conscious not only of the duplicity of those who use language but also of the duplicity of language itself.

Imagery

As You Like It abounds in natural imagery. Although there are no extended set piece descriptions, there are many references to trees and shrubs, running brooks, animals, various aspects of cultivation, and the weather that together sustain the forest setting and its atmosphere.

References to the weather and the seasons also suggest the theme of time, and indeed may point to one of its hidden messages. The last of the simple country songs sung by the pages, 'It was a lover and his lass' (V.3.15) with its reference to spring time and the prime, where previous songs have mentioned winter and foul weather, forms a fitting prelude to the conclusion in which the young couples are to marry in the prime of their life and make good use of their time while they may.

There are many references to time making up what may be called a pattern of thematic imagery. Some notable instances are as follows: the Duke and his followers are said 'to fleet the time carelessly as they did in the golden world' (I.1.111). Celia says that she likes the forest 'And willingly could waste my time in it' (II.4.92). There is Touchstone's disquisition on time as reported by Jaques (II.7.22ff). Orlando remarks to Rosalind that there is no clock in the forest (III.2.292) which prompts Rosalind's extended disquisition on aspects of time. She tells Orlando that time will test his words (IV.1.184).

PART FOUR

TEXTUAL ANALYSIS

TEXT 1 (II.4.1–72)

Having witnessed his victory over the wrestler Charles, Rosalind has fallen in love with Orlando. Banished from the court of Duke Frederick, Rosalind and her cousin Celia who has decided to accompany her are seen here for the first time in their disguise as Ganymede and Aliena in the Forest of Arden.

Enter ROSALIND *as* GANYMEDE, CELIA *as* ALIENA, *and the* CLOWN, *alias* TOUCHSTONE

ROSALIND: O Jupiter, how weary are my spirits!

TOUCHSTONE: I care not for my spirits, if my legs were not weary.

ROSALIND: I could find in my heart to disgrace my man's apparel, and to cry like a woman, but I must comfort the weaker vessel, as doublet-and-hose ought to show itself courageous to petticoat: therefore courage, good Aliena!

CELIA: I pray you, bear with me, I cannot go no further.

TOUCHSTONE: For my part, I had rather bear with you than bear you: yet I should bear no cross if I did bear you, for I think you have no money in your purse.

ROSALIND: Well, this is the Forest of Arden.

TOUCHSTONE: Ay, now I am in Arden, the more fool I. When I was at home I was in a better place, but travellers must be content.

Enter CORIN *and* SILVIUS

ROSALIND: Ay, be so, good Touchstone. – Look you, who comes here:
A young man and an old in solemn talk.

CORIN: That is the way to make her scorn you still.

SILVIUS: O Corin, that thou knewest how I do love her!

CORIN: I partly guess, for I have loved ere now.

SILVIUS: No, Corin, being old thou canst not guess,
Though in thy youth thou wast as true a lover
As ever sighed upon a midnight pillow.
But if thy love were ever like to mine –
As sure I think did never man love so –
How many actions most ridiculous
Hast thou been drawn to by thy fantasy?

CORIN: Into a thousand that I have forgotten.

SILVIUS: O, thou didst then never love so heartily.
If thou rememberest not the slightest folly
That ever love did make thee run into,
Thou hast not loved.
Or if thou hast not sat as I do now,
Wearing thy hearer in thy mistress' praise,
Thou hast not loved.
Or if thou hast not broke from company
Abruptly, as my passion now makes me,
Thou hast not loved.
O Phebe, Phebe, Phebe!

ROSALIND: Alas, poor shepherd, searching of thy wound,
I have by hard adventure found mine own.

TOUCHSTONE: And I mine. I remember when I was in love I broke my sword upon a stone and bid him take that for coming a-night to Jane Smile, and I remember the kissing of her batler and the cow's dugs that her pretty chopt hands had milked; and I remember the wooing of a peascod instead of her, from whom I took two cods and, giving her them again, said with weeping tears, 'Wear these for my sake.' We that are true lovers run into strange capers; but as all is mortal in nature, so is all nature in love mortal in folly.

ROSALIND: Thou speakest wiser than thou art ware of.

TOUCHSTONE: Nay, I shall ne'er be ware of mine own wit
till I break my shins against it.

ROSALIND: Jove, jove! This shepherd's passion
Is much upon my fashion.

TOUCHSTONE: And mine, but it grows something stale with me.

CELIA: I pray you, one of you question yond man
If he for gold will give us any food;
I faint almost to death.

TOUCHSTONE: Holla, you clown!

ROSALIND: Peace, fool, he's not thy kinsman.

CORIN: Who calls?

TOUCHSTONE: Your betters, sir.

CORIN: Else are they very wretched.

ROSALIND: Peace, I say. Good even to you, friend.

CORIN: And to you, gentle sir, and to you all.

ROSALIND: I prithee, shepherd, if that love or gold
Can in this desert place buy entertainment,
Bring us where we may rest ourselves and feed.
Here's a young maid with travail much oppressed,
And faints for succour.

In this scene for the first time we experience the effect of the disguise on the protagonists. At court, Rosalind, though witty, had been subordinate to her cousin Celia, daughter of the ruling Duke. Celia had taken the initiative and had as much to say and do as Rosalind. Here in the Forest of Arden, the roles are immediately reversed. Disguised as a man, Rosalind takes the leading role: she takes the initiative and the whole focus is upon her. She dominates the action with Celia who is now thoroughly subordinated. Rosalind is conscious of the demands of her new role about which she makes a joke; as a woman, her weariness after the journey might well have disposed her to tears but her disguise as a man requires the masculine behaviour to go with it. Men must not cry but comfort 'the weaker vessel'. The use of articles of clothing ('doublet and hose' and 'petticoat') to signify gender roles is witty and occurs elsewhere in the play. When Celia is slow in naming the person who has been writing the verses that she has found in the forest, Rosalind asks 'Dost thou think, though I am caparisoned like a man, I have doublet and hose in my disposition?' (III.2.188–90) Later, after Rosalind has been taunting Orlando and defaming the female sex, Celia upbraids her with the remark 'We must have your doublet and hose plucked over your head' (IV.1.187–8).

The opening section of this extract like much of the play is in prose but with the approach of the shepherds Corin and Silvius, 'A young man and an old in solemn talk', Rosalind utters two lines that are usually printed as verse, marking a change of register to the more solemn discourse of love. The shepherds are lower on the social scale than even the disguised protagonists so that this change has nothing to do with the distinction between courtiers and country people but is a change in literary register from witty free-moving comedy to the formalities of love in its **pastoral** mode. It later becomes apparent that the aged Corin is conceived as a realistic shepherd, but the young Silvius throughout is the plaintive and passionate love-sick shepherd, a literary type that featured in many classical and Renaissance pastorals. The style of his speech is high-flown and formal, marked by the refrain of the pathetic half line 'Thou hast not loved'. The literary type he resembles represents the young man extravagantly and egotistically absorbed in an unrequited love (he is scorned) which he believes to be unique. In the word 'fantasy', desire, is a latent recognition of the role played by the imagination in love. Yet Silvius is allowed some self-knowledge. From the questions that he asks Corin it is evident that he knows that this love has involved him in ridiculous actions and in folly.

The dramatic effect of this overheard encounter is to lead Rosalind to an awareness, expressed after Silvius and Corin have departed, that in the 'wound' of the shepherd she finds her own hurt, that is, she feels the same painful longing (for Orlando). Shakespeare thus establishes her feelings indirectly and presents her as a character who is capable of self-analysis. The folly of romantic love, a central conception upon which the whole play is built, is here associated primarily with Silvius, and anything ridiculous about romantic love is diverted from the heroine to him.

Rosalind's self-knowledge is echoed in the response of Touchstone who is given by far the longest speech in this scene. His earthy matter-of-fact prose is in marked contrast to the poetic interlude featuring the two shepherds. His presence before and after the interlude helps to frame it and is a key element in the presentation of the love theme here and elsewhere. If love is folly, then what better dramatic embodiment of this could there be than to involve the fool very closely in comment on the action? His perspective diversifies the scene and provides a counterpoint to its romantic sentiment. His earthiness is apparent from the start of the scene. Where Rosalind complains of tired spirits, Touchstone comments that he cares not for spirits but for tired legs. His **wordplay** in response to Celia's plea that they bear with her shows him to be a very material fool, one who is used to soliciting payment for his wit. He is less than charmed by the spirit of Arden: 'When I was at home I was in a better place'. Out of place in this setting, he sounds a contrary discordant note that prevents the composition from becoming too sweetly cloying.

After the allusions to romantic love in the sighs of Silvius on his midnight pillow and the recognition of Rosalind of its wounding power, the images and language of Touchstone offer a sharp contrast and humorous counterpoint. Jane Smile with her chapped hands and her 'batler', a wooden paddle for beating clothes, may be a country girl but is far from being the idealised beauty of the pastoral shepherdess. The image of the 'cow's dugs' again brings us down to earth. The wooing with a peascod may be a quaint country custom but given the repetition in 'two cods' (which can mean testicles) peascod may suggest codpiece, peascod transposed. There is probably bawdy significance in his opening remark about the breaking of the sword upon a stone too. The lyrical pastoral mood therefore does not survive Touchstone's bawdy wordplay.

Yet it can be said that the fool is making the same thematic point about love. His phrase 'We that are true lovers run into strange capers' echoes that of Silvius earlier 'If thou rememberest not the slightest folly / That ever love did make thee run into, / Thou hast not loved'. And the witty and neatly expressed maxim with which he concludes this speech could be said to encapsulate the major theme of the comedy, 'but as all is mortal in nature, so is all nature in love mortal in folly', that is, abundant in folly. Touchstone's language and comment are therefore a variation of the main theme.

The truth of the maxim is recognised by Rosalind who caps what Touchstone has said with her comment, 'Thou speakest wiser than thou art ware of', referring to Touchstone's ignorance of her passion for Orlando. As Shakespeare had enhanced the wisdom of his heroine by making her recognise the truth of her own condition in the experience of Silvius so he makes her absorb and go beyond the insights of the wise fool in acknowledging the truth about the nature of love. The truth itself may be commonplace but the incorporation of it into the developing action is artfully contrived to enhance the heroine.

The subversive character of Touchstone's **wit** is reflected in his punning reply to Rosalind. He will only be wary of his wit when he is surprised or injured by its consequences. Intellect dominates at the expense of feeling; the professional joker is detached from his own jokes. In this he differs from Rosalind with whom he shares a delight in punning. A more courteous and feeling character, Rosalind rebukes him for his rude reference to the shepherd as a country clown. Her smart reply 'he's not thy kinsman' turns the tables on Touchstone though it does not entirely put him in his place as his reply to Corin, 'Your betters, sir' is still patronising. Corin, however, continues the play of wit, whether consciously or unconsciously, as he understands betters not in the sense of social superiors but those who are more fortunate. Touchstone therefore not only jokes himself but prompts verbal humour in those around him. The most routine encounters (here a request for food) are enlivened by the constant wit and wordplay. This scene, in which wit and wordplay predominate and provide a frame within which the simpler language of love is shown to be slightly absurd, may be regarded as a microcosm of the play as a whole.

TEXT 2 (II.5 AND II.6)

Rosalind and Celia, weary and faint for lack of nourishment after their journey from the court into the Forest of Arden, have just made arrangements for their material well-being through the good offices of Corin. In another part of the forest, Amiens, one of the Duke's lords and his musician, has encountered Jaques for whom the Duke is looking.

Enter AMIENS, JAQUES *and others*

AMIENS: (*sings*)

Under the greenwood tree,
Who loves to lie with me,
And turn his merry note
Unto the sweet bird's throat:
Come hither, come hither, come hither.
Here shall he see
No enemy
But winter and rough weather.

JAQUES: More, more, I prithee, more.

AMIENS: It will make you melancholy, Monsieur Jaques.

JAQUES: I thank it. More, I prithee, more. I can suck melancholy out of a song, as a weasel sucks eggs. More, I prithee, more.

AMIENS: My voice is ragged, I know I cannot please you.

JAQUES: I do not desire you to please me, I do desire you to sing. Come, more, another stanzo. Call you 'em 'stanzos'?

AMIENS: What you will, Monsieur Jaques.

JAQUES: Nay, I care not for their names, they owe me nothing. Will you sing?

AMIENS: More at your request than to please myself.

JAQUES: Well then, if ever I thank any man, I'll thank you; but that they call 'compliment' is like th'encounter of two dog-apes, and when a man thanks me heartily, methinks I have given him a penny and he renders me the beggarly thanks. Come, sing; and you that will not, hold your tongues.

AMIENS: Well, I'll end the song. – Sirs, cover the while: the Duke will drink under this tree. – He hath been all this day to look you.

JAQUES: And I have been all this day to avoid him. He is too disputable for my company: I think of as many matters as he, but I give heaven thanks, and make no boast of them. Come, warble, come.

ALL TOGETHER: (*sing*)

Who doth ambition shun,
And loves to live i'th'sun,
Seeking the food he eats,
And pleased with what he gets:
Come hither, come hither, come hither.
Here shall he see
No enemy
But winter and rough weather.

JAQUES: I'll give you a verse to this note, that I made yesterday in despite of my invention.

AMIENS: And I'll sing it.

JAQUES: Thus it goes:

If it do come to pass
That any man turn ass,
Leaving his wealth and ease,
A stubborn will to please:
Ducdame, ducdame, ducdame.
Here shall he see
Gross fools as he,
An if he will come to me.

AMIENS: What's that 'ducdame'?

JAQUES: 'Tis a Greek invocation, to call fools into a circle. I'll go sleep, if I can; if I cannot, I'll rail against all the first-born of Egypt.

AMIENS: And I'll go seek the duke; his banquet is prepared.

Exeunt

II.6

Enter ORLANDO *and* ADAM

ADAM: Dear master, I can go no further. O, I die for food. Here lie I down and measure out my grave. Farewell, kind master.

ORLANDO: Why, how now, Adam, no greater heart in thee? Live a little, comfort a little, cheer thyself a little. If this uncouth forest yield anything savage, I will either be food for it or bring it for food to thee. Thy conceit is nearer death than thy powers. (*Raising him*) For my sake be comfortable; hold death a while at the arm's end. I will here be with thee presently, and if I bring thee not something to eat, I will give thee leave to die; but if thou diest before I come, thou art a mocker of my labour. Well said! Thou lookest cheerly, and I'll be with thee quickly. Yet thou liest in the bleak air. Come, I will bear thee to some shelter, and thou shalt not die for lack of a dinner, if there live anything in this desert. Cheerly, good Adam!

Exeunt

This scene contains the first of the play's celebrated songs written in a simple unpretentious style suitable here for the celebration of the simple county life, without strife ('No enemy / But winter and rough weather') and free from ambition. The first verse is a happy evocation of the carefree green life of nature in the forest. It is addressed to those who respond merrily to the sweet song of the birds, that is, to those who are happy to embrace simple pleasures in appreciation of natural beauty. Despite this, nature is not wholly idealised for there is mention of winter and rough weather, but the clear implication is that however hostile the elements may be this hostility is as nothing compared with the vicissitudes of human life in the civilised world of the court. In the second verse, living in the sun has a figurative as well as literal meaning evocative of a happy and blessed life lived in the open air where one might seek one's own food and be content with the result, an alternative to the life of ambition and social success in which the seeking of food is a menial task left to others and where the highest value is put on the most exquisite luxury. Amiens's song embodies the simple philosophy that underpins life in the forest. When after singing he gives directions that a table be set, for 'the Duke will drink under this tree', the song and its philosophy is clearly associated with the Duke.

The placing of this song is highly significant. It might have come after the Duke's earlier praise of the virtues of life in the forest in contrast to the dangers of the envious court (II.1.1ff). There the Duke's idyll is immediately followed by something that to some extent upsets and modifies it: one of the Duke's lords tells how Jaques laments the killing of the deer and calls the Duke and his followers usurpers in the forest. Here the song with its simple message and the mood it creates is similarly disrupted again by Jaques who has a lengthy altercation with the singer, Amiens, and then sings a verse of his own composition which is a parody of the song and reverses its sentiments.

After the singing of the opening verse our attention is diverted from the sentiments of the song by the unwillingness of Amiens to sing a second verse despite the insistent pleas of Jaques. The song is not particularly sad, indeed its content demands that its singing conveys the 'merry note' of its third line, but Amiens tells Jaques that it will make him melancholy. This pleases Jaques. He enjoys being morbid. His explanatory remark that he can 'suck melancholy out of a song as a weasel sucks eggs' suggests an almost perverse determination to indulge his 'humour'. The country image is vivid but the weasel is a destructive and quarrelsome predator (there are no weasels in idyllic literary **pastorals**). Amiens feels that he cannot please him and this proves to be the case. The mood created by the opening verse is quickly dissipated by the reluctance of Amiens and the tenor of Jaques's remarks.

These remarks help to establish his character (though we have heard about him before, this is his first appearance on stage). His use of the Italian 'stanzo' shows his cultivation and knowledge; perhaps he is showing off or mocking the affectation of foreign terms. There is certainly an element of show and mockery in his witty rejoinder to Amiens's non-committal reply with its learned quibble on *names* as signatures on a legal document acknowledging a debt. His thanks to Amiens, is delivered somewhat obliquely; 'if ever I thank any man' suggests a surly and ungrateful disposition. He justifies his lack of grace with a little homily on the nature of 'compliment', polite manners or social niceties. These put him in mind of the behaviour of baboons, in this context a demeaning image, and his own response to the expression of hearty thanks is revealing in its suspicion and cynicism.

In the light of this exchange with Amiens and the character that it establishes, Jaques's reasons for avoiding the Duke who has been seeking his company all day seem slightly suspect. He says the Duke is too 'disputable', argumentative, yet he seems to derive pleasure from arguments himself; he further says that he thinks of as many matters as the Duke but, thank heaven, he is not a show-off. This does not entirely ring true. There is something showy in his character and **wit**. From his dealing with Amiens and others it seems that Jaques is of superior social status; he can therefore give vent to expressions of feeling that must be restrained in the presence of the Duke.

His parody of Amiens's song offers a contrary view. Anyone who voluntarily leaves his wealth and ease is an ass and as foolish as those now in the forest (who are not there voluntarily but who are making the best of their lot). It is one of the functions of the role of Jaques to be a contrary character who offers an alternative perspective. His alternative view of life in the forest is not endorsed elsewhere but nor is its author ridiculed. As a melancholic figure in a comedy he stands apart, but he is not made to renounce his introspective melancholy in the happy ending. In an eighteenth-century adaptation of the play, Celia married Jaques rather than Oliver. Shakespeare, however, did not seek to convert him from his humour but diverts it without punishment or ridicule; Jaques is allowed to find his own alternative happiness in a religious life of withdrawal in the final movement of the play.

His final mysterious remarks in this scene, however, complete the impression of prickly aloofness that he has given previously. Baffled by the word 'ducdame', Amiens asks him to explain its meaning. Jaques's learned explanation has baffled editors of the play; no one has been able to track the word down. Is it, therefore, deliberately nonsensical? The word has acted as a cue in some productions for the other lords in this scene to come round in a circle, thus becoming the circle of fools that Jaques is mocking. He certainly seems to be toying with his audience and showing off his intellectual superiority. His final sally, that if he cannot sleep he will 'rail against the firstborn of Egypt' alludes to the biblical story in *Exodus* 12:29–33 where the death of the first-born Egyptians caused a great cry in the night, thus waking everybody up. As a result of their death the Pharaoh allowed the captive Israelites to leave Egypt; when they discovered how hard life was in the wilderness they began murmuring against Moses and wishing that they had died along with the Egyptians. The allusion is therefore complex, and perhaps expresses his discontent with life in the forest (a wilderness, as far as he is concerned) in terms that would have appealed to the learned wits in the audience. What cannot be missed, however is the tone of the remark and the directness of 'I'll rail against'; rail is a strong word containing ridicule, abuse and criticism and general grumbling.

As a character who on his own admission rails against the world, Jaques is a variation of a familiar type on the Elizabethan stage, the '**malcontent**' or discontented man. But while the type makes him recognisably familiar, it is the variation that makes him interesting. This melancholy alienated intellectual, in whose mouth Shakespeare put one of his most famous speeches ('All the world's a stage' (II.7.140ff), has exerted a peculiar fascination, partly because we do not really know the cause of his alienation. There is something mysteriously incomprehensible about him. His is certainly the part in the play that offers the most scope for male actors and there have been almost as many different Jaques as Hamlets in the history of Shakespeare productions.

Not much in this scene may seem to advance the plot, but Amiens's direction, delivered almost as an aside, that a table be set for the Duke and the indication at the end that he is off to find the Duke as his meal has been prepared sets the scene for what follows. In a different part of the forest Rosalind and Celia had previously been concerned for the provision of food and shelter and in the brief scene that follows, the need for food and shelter is an urgent necessity for Orlando and Adam. The Forest of Arden is not quite the paradise of classical pastoral where the necessities of life are all taken care of without any labour on the part of its inhabitants. At least it is not so for those entering it for the first time. Orlando, whose good nature is tested in the forest and not found wanting, finds it to be 'uncouth', a 'desert' (that is, a wilderness) where the air is 'bleak'. And it nearly causes the death of Adam. The song of Amiens and Jaques's response to it and the suffering of Adam which requires Orlando to act constitute a complicated sequence of greatly

TEXT 2 continued

varied parts in which the action, mood and movement of the play is diversified and extended.

TEXT 3 (V.4.35–104)

In the final scene of the play, Rosalind, still in disguise as Ganymede, has just promised to unite the Duke with his daughter and Orlando with his lover. As Rosalind and Celia depart to change out of their disguises, Orlando and the Duke briefly wonder whether the youth will be able to achieve what he has promised. At this point Touchstone enters with Audrey to the amusement of Jaques who shows off the clown to the Duke.

> JAQUES: There is sure another flood toward, and these couples are coming to the ark. Here comes a pair of very strange beasts, which in all tongues are called fools.
>
> TOUCHSTONE: Salutation and greeting to you all!
>
> JAQUES: Good my lord, bid him welcome: this is the motley-minded gentleman that I have so often met in the forest. He hath been a courtier, he swears.
>
> TOUCHSTONE: If any man doubt that, let him put me to my purgation. I have trod a measure, I have flattered a lady, I have been politic with my friend, smooth with mine enemy, I have undone three tailors, I have had four quarrels, and like to have fought one.
>
> JAQUES: And how was that ta'en up?
>
> TOUCHSTONE: Faith, we met, and found the quarrel was upon the seventh cause.
>
> JAQUES: How seventh cause? – Good my lord, like this fellow.
>
> DUKE: I like him very well.
>
> TOUCHSTONE: God 'ild you, sir, I desire you of the like. I press in here, sir amongst the rest of the country

opulatives, to swear and to forswear, according as marriage binds and blood breaks. A poor virgin, sir, an ill-favoured thing, sir, but mine own, a poor humour of mine, sir, to take that that no man else will. Rich honesty dwells like a miser, sir, in a poor house, as your pearl in your foul oyster.

DUKE: By my faith, he is very swift and sententious.

TOUCHSTONE: According to the fool's bolt, sir, and such dulcet diseases.

JAQUES: But for the seventh cause. How did you find the quarrel on the seventh cause?

TOUCHSTONE: Upon a lie seven times removed. – Bear your body more seeming Audrey. – As thus, sir. I did dislike the cut of a certain courtier's beard. He sent me word, if I said his beard was not cut well, he was in the mind it was: this is called the Retort Courteous. If I sent him word again it was not well cut, he would send me word he cut it to please himself: this is called the Quip Modest. If again 'it was not well cut', he disabled my judgement: this is called the Reply Churlish. If again 'it was not well cut', he would answer, I spake not true: this is called the Reproof Valiant. If again 'it was not well cut', he would say I lie: this is called the Countercheck Quarrelsome: and so to Lie Circumstantial and the Lie Direct.

JAQUES: And how oft did you say his beard was not well cut?

TOUCHSTONE: I durst go no further than the Lie Circumstantial, nor he durst not give me the Lie Direct. And so we measured swords and parted.

JAQUES: Can you nominate in order now the degrees of the lie?

TOUCHSTONE: O sir, we quarrel in print, by the book, as you have books for good manners. I will name you the

> degrees. The first, the Retort Courteous; the second, the Quip Modest; the third, the Reply Churlish; the fourth, the Reproof Valiant; the fifth, the Countercheck Quarrelsome; the sixth, the Lie with Circumstance; the seventh, the Lie Direct. All these you may avoid but the Lie Direct; and you may avoid that too, with an 'If'. I knew when seven justices could not take up a quarrel, but when the parties were met themselves, one of them thought but of an 'If': as, 'If you said so, then I said so'; and they shook hands and swore brothers. Your 'If' is the only peace-maker; much virtue in 'If'.
>
> JAQUES: Is not this a rare fellow, my lord? He's as good at anything, and yet a fool.
>
> DUKE: He uses his folly like a stalking-horse, and under the presentation of that, he shoots his wit.

In the plot the scene fills in time while Rosalind and Celia take off their disguises, but the exchange between these two principal 'commentators', who in their different ways put a worldly and sometimes cynical perspective on the romantic mood and theme of the play, provides a necessary element of emotional balance to the romantic ending, providing a comic interlude in the serious business of the final act in which the lovers are paired off and order is restored. Thus the mixture of **wit** and **romance** is maintained to the end.

Jaques's opening description of Touchstone and Audrey as 'a pair of very strange beasts which in all tongues are called fools' draws attention to the comic incongruity of the couple, only too apparent in the earlier scene (Act III Scene 3) in which the sophisticated Touchstone, the court jester, had wooed the simple and unsophisticated country-girl Audrey. A good production will bring out this incongruity in their visual appearance, different as they are from one another and from the other lovers and exiled courtiers in whose midst we find them. Audrey is silent in the scene and Touchstone's direction to her 'Bear your body more seeming, Audrey' is the only reminder of her presence in the text. This remark allows more visual comedy in Audrey's 'unseeming' deportment. The unseemly incongruity of this pair of lovers gives a comic dimension to the romantic theme and their presence at the end acts as a kind of safety valve for the audience's cynicism as the unrealistic happy ending is contrived.

Jaques had encountered Touchstone in the forest previously and spoken of him in rapturous terms to the Duke (Act II Scene 7). In their only other scene together (Act III Scene 3) they had been at cross-purposes, with Jaques intervening to prevent Touchstone marrying Audrey. Here, after his initial mocking introduction, Jaques delightedly acts as a 'feed', plying Touchstone with questions to draw out his wit to show him off to the Duke. Jaques calls him 'motley-minded', alluding to the variegated dress of the court fool but expressing a quality of Touchstone's character and role: he is a variegated character of no fixed colour. In this scene he is as critical of the court as he was earlier of the country when debating with Corin (Act III Scene 2). So much that he says is for the effect of the moment because it is the role of the fool to be instantly entertaining.

Touchstone's wit is directed good-humouredly at himself when he talks of his 'poor humour … to take that no man else will' but is primarily directed at courtly failings. It is a clever and disarming touch that his criticism of these failings should be presented as a catalogue of his own hollow achievements as a courtier. He has danced stately measures, flattered a lady, been 'politic' (crafty) with his friend, and 'smooth' (fair-speaking) with his enemy. In his satire, courtiers have concern only for style and manners at the expense of substance and truth. His witty sallies are therefore not unconnected with a central thematic preoccupation of the play: criticism of the court.

Further extravagance of style, triviality and dishonesty are suggested in the joke about 'undoing', that is, bankrupting, three tailors, where the choice of 'undoing' is particularly witty in the context of tailoring which has much to do with doing things up. The climax of this quickly delivered catalogue, is cleverly signalled by the advance in number from three tailors to four quarrels; the sting of the satire comes in the surprising retreat of the anticlimactic final clause 'and like to have fought one'. A true knight (and the courtly ideal of the Renaissance is an extension of the medieval chivalric ideal) pursues his quarrels honourably to the point of duelling.

The point of the rest of Touchstone's discourse 'upon the seventh cause' leading up to the 'Lie Direct' is to satirise courtiers who wish to appear to go through the motions of belligerence but actually engage in verbal skirmishing to keep up appearances because in fact they are afraid to fight. It is all about courtly evasion of the truth. Yet the subtlety of Touchstone's anarchic wit is such that these old codes of honour are themselves made ridiculous. Even to an Elizabethan audience to whom the various terms might have suggested stages in a contemporary manual of etiquette for disputation, Touchstone's discourse must have sounded absurd relating as it does to the trivial circumstance of an insult about the cut of a beard. It sounds like nonsense that almost verges on sense, or it seems like sense twisted into nonsense. It is a feature of Touchstone's language throughout the play that it never quite settles consistently to any one line but dances along a very fine and sometimes unsettling line between sense and nonsense so that we cannot always be quite sure where we are.

Touchstone's language, therefore, in this extract, like that of the courtiers he is mocking has its own style, though in highlighting their hollowness it is not without substance. He refers to Audrey as 'a poor virgin' and then makes a moral point that, if we take it seriously, goes some way to explain his choice of the 'ill-favoured' (ugly) Audrey for a bride : 'Rich honesty dwells like a miser, sir, in a poor house, as your pearl in your foul oyster'. He is unflattering and direct about her looks and values her inner moral worth, so that he represents himself as the reverse of the smooth-tongued and flattering courtiers he has been mocking. There is a direct honesty about his words and the views he expresses that may be said to compensate for his lack of courteous gallantry towards Audrey.

In his view of relations between the sexes, Touchstone shows no awareness of the spiritual dimension. He is an earthy sensualist who is marrying for sex. Accordingly when he is talking about marriage at the beginning, his language is peppered with double entendres of a bawdy suggestiveness. The most obvious is his use of 'country copulatives' for couples in the country, which certainly suggests copulation and perhaps also brings with it a reference to the female sexual organ. Commentators suggest that there is a reference to premature ejaculation in the phrase 'the fool's bolt' and to venereal disease in the ironic phrase 'dulcet diseases'. Yet for all this there is a beguiling beauty in the neat precision of his **wordplay**. The word 'copulatives' not only suggests copulation but also wittily introduces a series of linguistic doubles, words and phrases joined together in opposition: 'to swear and to forswear, according as marriage binds and blood breaks'. Nor is there anything redundant in these doubles; Touchstone's utterances are always full of matter (Jaques had earlier called him a 'material fool' – III.3.29). Here is a reminder of one of the great truths of human experience: the dichotomy between our good intentions and the pull of the flesh. There is a further neat **antithesis** between 'Rich honesty' dwelling 'in a poor house' succinctly encapsulated in the simile 'as your pearl in your foul oyster'. No wonder that the Duke at this point calls him 'swift and sententious', quick-witted and full of maxims.

His language in the rest of the extract continues to be precise and formal. In response to Jaques's question about the degrees of the lie, he explains his meaning and purpose: 'O sir, we quarrel by the book, as you have books for good manners'. Commentators cite a number of contemporary books on manners and on duelling including Vincentio Saviolo's *His Practise of the Rapier and Dagger* (1594–5) which contains a discourse on 'the giving and receiving of a lie'. In reproducing at some length the jargon of such books, Touchstone reduces it and its adherents, those who do things 'by the book', to absurdity. The absurdity has point, prompting the Duke's insight: 'He uses his folly as a stalking-horse, and under the presentation of that he shoots his wit'. This is in itself a clever remark, for the stalking horse (behind which a hunter hid so as to get near to his prey) might be a real horse or an imitation one; we are never quite sure with Touchstone about the extent to which his folly is natural or assumed. But what is certain is that the folly is a display or semblance 'a presentation' through which Touchstone exercises an intelligence and imaginative talent, his 'wit'. What the Duke says of the Shakespearean fool might with equal propriety be said of the fool's creator in the larger context of the comedy.

Part five

Background

William shakespeare

There are no personal records of Shakespeare's life. Official documents and occasional references to him enable us to draw the main outline of his public life but his private life remains hidden. What we do know can be quickly summarised.

Shakespeare was born into a well-to-do family in the market town of Stratford-upon-Avon in Warwickshire, where he was baptised, in Holy Trinity Church, on 26 April 1564. His father, John Shakespeare, was a prosperous glover and leather merchant who became a person of some importance in the town: in 1565 he was elected an alderman of the town, and in 1568 he became high bailiff (or mayor) of Stratford, In 1557 he had married Mary Arden, Their third child (of eight) and eldest son, William, learned to read and write at the primary (or 'petty') school in Stratford and then, it seems probable, attended the local grammar school, where he would have studied Latin, history, logic and rhetoric. In November 1582 William, then aged eighteen, married Anne Hathaway, who was twenty six years old. They had a daughter, Susanna, in May 1583, and twins, Hamnet and Judith in 1585.

Shakespeare next appears in the historical record in 1592 when he was mentioned as a London actor and playwright in a pamphlet by the dramatist Robert Greene. During the next twenty years, he continued to live in London, regularly visiting his wife and family in Stratford. He continued to act, but his chief fame was as a dramatist. From 1594 he wrote exclusively for the Lord Chamberlain's Men, which rapidly became the leading dramatic company and from 1603 enjoyed the patronage of James I as the King's Men. His plays were extremely popular and he became a shareholder in his theatre company. He was able to buy lands around Stratford and a large house in the town, to which he retired about 1611. He died there on April 23 1616 and was buried in Holy Trinity Church on 25 April.

Shakespeare's other works

Between the late 1580s and 1613 Shakespeare wrote thirty-seven plays and contributed to some by other dramatists. An exact chronology of the plays is not possible; the dates below give the earliest and latest dates for their writing and performance.

He began by rewriting earlier plays and working plotlines inspired by the classics. *The Comedy of Errors* (1590–4), for example, is based upon *The Brothers Menaechmi* by the Roman playwright Plautus. His earlier plays are comedies and histories for the most part. Among the comedies, those that may be juxtaposed most fruitfully with *As You Like It* (1598–1600) are *Love's Labour's Lost* (1588–97) which has witty women who mock the courtly wooing of their male admirers, *A Midsummer Night's Dream* (1594–8) a comic romantic fantasy with a woodland setting on the theme of the folly, instability and lunacy of the state of love, *Much Ado about Nothing* (1598–1600) which has a witty and realistic heroine in every way the equal of her suitor, and *Twelfth Night* (1600–2) with the use of disguise and cross-dressing and the inclusion of a professional fool.

His English history plays, completed with *Henry V* in 1599, tell an epic story which examines how modern England came into being through the conflicts of the fifteenth-century Wars of the Roses (from the emblems of the two factions of the British Royal family, the white rose of York and the red rose of Lancaster) which brought the Tudors to the throne. The two parts of *Henry IV* (1596–8), in which one of his most popular comic characters Falstaff appears, have a mixture of comic and serious scenes and public and private worlds. Although these scenes are more separate and are not harmonised as the serious and comic elements are in *As You Like It* its flexible generic mix provides an apposite comparison.

As the new century begins a new note is detectable. Plays such as *Troilus and Cressida* (1601–2) and *Measure for Measure* (1603–4), in which there is a perceptible tension between the disparate elements of comedy and tragedy, evoke complex responses. Because of their generic uncertainty and ambivalent tone such works are sometimes referred to as 'problem plays'. *Hamlet* (1600–1), *Othello* (1602–4), *King Lear* (1605–6) and *Macbeth* (1605–6), together with the Roman plays *Julius Caesar*

(1598–1600), *Antony and Cleopatra* (1606–8) and *Coriolanus* (1605–10) constitute his main tragic period.. His last plays, often called the late **romances**, do not have tragic resolutions; they end harmoniously in forgiveness and reconciliation. Of these, *The Tempest* (1609–11) which is set on an island away from the court, has a usurpation of a younger brother by an older and ends harmoniously in marriage has most in common with *As You Like It*.

Historical background

Shakespeare's early career is part of the great flowering in literature and culture that occurred in the late Elizabethan age, given impetus by the growth in national self-confidence resulting from the defeat of the Spanish Armada in 1588. This flowering is itself part of a wider movement rejuvenating European culture which since the nineteenth century has been known by the term *Renaissance*. Meaning literally *rebirth* it denotes a revival and redirection of artistic and intellectual endeavour which began in Italy in the fourteenth century in the poetry of Petrarch (1304–74). It spread gradually northwards across Europe, and is first detectable in England in the early sixteenth century in the writings of the scholar and statesman Sir Thomas More (1478–1535) and in the poetry of Sir Thomas Wyatt (1503–42) and Henry Howard, Earl of Surrey (c.1517–47), all associated with the court of Henry VIII. Its keynote was a curiosity in thought which challenged old assumptions and traditions. To the innovative spirit of the Renaissance, the preceding ages appeared dully unoriginal and conformist.

That spirit was fuelled by the rediscovery of many classical texts and the culture of Greece and Rome. This fostered a confidence in human reason and in human potential which, in every sphere, challenged old convictions. The discovery of America and its peoples (Columbus had sailed in 1492) demonstrated that the world was a larger and stranger place than had hitherto been thought. The cosmological speculation of Copernicus (1473–1543, later confirmed by Galileo, 1564–1642) that the sun, not the earth was the centre of our planetary system challenged the centuries-old belief that the earth and human beings were at the centre of the cosmos. The pragmatic political philosophy of Machiavelli

(1469–1527) seemed to cut politics free from its traditional link with morality by permitting statesmen any means which secured the desired end. And the religious movements we know collectively as the Reformation broke with the Church of Rome and set the individual conscience, not ecclesiastical authority, at the centre of the religious life. Nothing, it seemed, was beyond questioning, nothing impossible.

Shakespeare's drama is innovative and challenging in exactly the way of the Renaissance. It interrogates (examines and asks questions of) the beliefs, assumptions and politics upon which Elizabethan society was founded. And though the plays always conclude in a restoration of order and stability, many critics are inclined to argue that their imaginative energy goes into subverting, rather than reinforcing, traditional values.

Literary background

Through the characters of Phebe and Silvius, the scornful mistress/shepherdess and rejected suitor/swain, Shakespeare is mocking the mode of courtly wooing prevalent in literary **pastoral**. But the attitudes, mannerisms and stylistic expressions of love that are ridiculed in *As You Like It* are equally to be found in the love sonnets of the Italian poet Petrarch (1304–74). This famous sonnet sequence which records Petrarch's extravagant adoration of his unattainable mistress Laura had been an influential model and continued to provide a point of reference for imitation in all love poets up to the time of Shakespeare and beyond. Shakespeare himself joined in the Renaissance fashion for sonneteering, but more than any English predecessor he consciously rejected its obvious conventions, notably in sonnet 131, often called the anti-**Petrarchan** sonnet, 'My mistress' eyes are nothing like the sun'. His sonnets are addressed not to the fair and virtuous idealised figure of the Petrarchan tradition but either to the 'dark' lady, who is dark in colouring and moral character by whom the poet seems to have been betrayed and whom he certainly is not courting, or to the poet's friend, who is courted, a beautiful young man. Nevertheless though the conventions are rejected, it may be said that the sonnets are often dependant upon the reader's knowledge of those conventions for their full effect. At any rate, what may be called Renaissance Petrarchanism is part of the literary background to *As You Like It*.

The immediate source is the prose **romance** *Rosalynde* (1590) by Thomas Lodge described and discussed in Critical Approaches. An earlier and more violent version of the same story is to be found in *The Tale of Gamelyn*, a mid-fourteenth-century poem found in manuscripts alongside Chaucer's *Canterbury Tales* but not now attributed to Chaucer. Courtly **pastoral romances** like *Rosalynde* were a kind of literature very popular in Elizabethan England, the most famous example being the long prose work of Sir Philip Sidney *The Countess of Pembroke's Arcadia* (1590).

The subtitle of *Rosalynde*, *Euphues His Legacie* suggests another antecedent of both Lodge and Shakespeare, *Euphues: The Anatomy of Wit* (1578) by John Lyly (c.1554–1606) which had made fashionable a new kind of prose style that came to be called **euphuism**. In Greek the adjectival form of the word means 'of good natural disposition', 'naturally clever'. In its connection with wit the word undergoes a perceptible metamorphosis, naturally clever expression becoming in fact highly arty and sophisticated as demonstrated in the opening description of the hero of *Euphues*:

> This young gallant, of more *wit* than *wealth*, and yet of more *wealth* than *wisdom*, *seeing himself inferior to none in pleasant conceits*, *thought himself superior to all in honest conditions*, insomuch that he deemed himself so apt to *all things*, that he gave himself almost to *nothing*, but practising of those things commonly which are incident to these sharp wits, fine phrases, smooth quipping, merry taunting, *using* jesting *without mean*, and *abusing* mirth *without measure*.

The young gallant, a person of some means and social position, is a bit of a conceited fellow, proud of his capacity for witty verbal display ('conceits') which he cultivates to the exclusion of all else and for its own sake, speaking entirely for effect and going beyond bounds in pursuit of humorous points. There is a moral judgement against him here but Lyly's own prose is itself witty, clever and full of pretty verbal effects. In the words in italics there is a deliberate and studied balancing of oppositions in both individual words and clauses underscored by patterns of **alliteration**. This antithetical style is very neat and precise even if it is taken almost to excess. To explain its impact, it would probably be necessary to set it against run-of-the-mill Elizabethan prose which is hard to read because its **syntax** is often muddled and its vocabulary uncouth. The style of *Euphues* is a learned style with many classical and Biblical allusions that assumes a learned audience and one that will appreciate its rhetorical display.

There is a fine appreciation of what this style might have meant to the Elizabethans and to Shakespeare in the criticism of Walter Pater (1839–94) writing about *Love's Labour's Lost* (1594), an earlier play in which Shakespeare mocks courtly fads and with which *As You Like It* has affinities:

> Play is often that about which people are most serious; and the humorist may observe how, under all love of playthings, there is almost always hidden an appreciation of something really engaging and delightful. This is true always of the toys of children; it is often true of the playthings of grown-up people, their vanities, their fopperies even, their lighter loves; the cynic would add their pursuit of fame. Certainly this is true without exception of the playthings of a past age, which to those who succeed it are always full of a pensive interest – old manners, old dresses, old houses. For what is called fashion in these matters occupies, in each age, much of the care of many of the most discerning people, furnishing them with a kind of mirror of their real inward refinements and their capacity for selection. Such modes or fashions are, at their best, an example of the artistic predominance of form over matter – of the manner of the doing of it over the thing done – and have a beauty of their own. It is so with that old euphuism of the Elizabethan age – that pride of dainty language and curious expression, which it is very easy to ridicule, which often made itself ridiculous, but which had below it a real sense of fitness and nicety; and which, as we see in this very play [*Love' Labour's Lost*], and still more clearly in the sonnets, had some fascination for the young Shakespeare himself ... This 'foppery' of Shakespeare's day had, then, its really delightful side, a quality in no sense 'affected', by which it satisfies a real instinct in our minds – the fancy so many of us have for an exquisite and curious skill in the use of words.
>
> (*Appreciations*, Macmillan, London and New York, 1889)

In *Love's Labour's Lost* the labour that is lost is all the conventional courtly love-play of the fashionable young gallants who go excitedly through the routine of sonneteering only to have their efforts mocked and thwarted by the women they are courting. The old-fashioned style of courtly wooing is also mocked in *As You Like It* though the labour of wooing is rewarded with a happy ending. Shakespeare takes delight in the old conventions of **pastoral**, **Petrarchanism** and **romance** and in the comparatively new fashion for **euphuistic** prose while fully appreciating their absurdity. This is the balance of attitudes described by Pater.

We may surmise that the young Shakespeare was dazzled by the fashionable literary world of the court when he came to London, but as a provincial from a Stratford family that had no connections with the ruling powers at court and a professional man of the theatre for whom drama had to be more than an elegant pastime, he could maintain a distance and detachment from the enthusiasms of the fashionable world. He could indulge himself and his audience and mock that indulgence at the same time. There is a remarkable balance of attitude in Shakespeare in contrast to, say, his great contemporary Ben Jonson (1572–1637), who on the one hand wrote **masques** for serious courtly entertainment and on the other wrote sharply satirical plays in which the affected manners of the court are mercilessly ridiculed.

Satire, at the time of the composition of *As You Like It* was all the rage. In fact in 1599 came the Bishops' ban on formal satire on the grounds that it encouraged sedition. Jaques defence of his satirical intent (that it is general and therefore only taxes the guilty (II.7.70)) may have some topical import. However, *As You Like It* is entirely safe and need cause no qualms for bishops then or now. In some respects in the context of its time the play is a conservative work in its literary affiliations. The avant garde in Shakespeare's day, poets like John Donne, (1571–1631), were turning their backs upon pastoral, Petrarchanism and romance much more radically than Shakespeare in *As You Like It*.

PART SIX

CRITICAL HISTORY AND BROADER PERSPECTIVES

EARLY RESPONSES

Although it is presumed that *As You Like It* was performed at the time of writing, there is no actual record of any such performance so that we have no means of knowing whether or not the play was a success or how it was received by its first audience.

All literature either can be said to reflect the taste of the period in which it is written or to be a critical response to that taste. As taste changes, the successes of one age may simply seem old fashioned and passé in succeeding times. There is little evidence that Shakespearean comedy made much of an impact in the seventeenth century; the bawdy and more realistic comedy of social manners in the period of the Restoration (beginning in 1660) when women acted for the first time on the English stage was of a very different in kind from what is offered in *As You Like It*, which was not revived in its entirety until 1740. At this time there is evidence that 'breeches parts', those which involved women disguised as men, had again become popular. Before that in 1723 *As You Like It* had been the basis of a play called *Love in a Forest* by Charles Johnson. He modernised much of the language and cut the parts of Touchstone, Audrey, William, Phebe and Corin. The speech on the sobbing deer was given to Jaques rather than to the First Lord. It is his good younger brother, who has come to tell Orlando of the wicked Oliver's death, whom Orlando rescues from the lioness. Celia marries Jaques at the end and the assembled company are entertained by a performance of *Pyramus and Thisbe* (from Shakespeare's *A Midsummer Night's Dream*).

In a general revival of interest in Shakespearean plays, *As You Like It* was amongst the most popular and most frequently produced in the second half of the eighteenth century and has remained so to this day. In the eighteenth century, Samuel Johnson (1709–84) remarked, 'Of this play the fable is wild and pleasing'. In the early nineteenth century, William Hazlitt (1778–1830) in his *Characters of Shakespeare's Plays* (1817) gave voice to the play's romantic appeal:

> Shakespeare has here converted the forest of Arden into another Arcadia, where they 'fleet the time carelessly, as they did in the golden world' [I.1.111]. It is the most ideal of any of this author's plays. It is a pastoral drama in which the interest arises more out of the sentiments and characters than out of the actions or situations. It is not what is done, but what is said, that claims our attention. Nursed in solitude, 'under the shade of melancholy boughs' [II.7.112] the imagination grows soft and delicate, and the wit runs riot in idleness, like a spoiled child that is never sent to school. Caprice and fancy reign and revel here, and stern necessity is banished in the court. The mild sentiments of humanity are strengthened with thought and leisure; the echo of cares and noise of the world strikes upon the ear of those 'who have felt them knowingly' [*Cymbeline*, III.3.46], softened by time and distance. 'They hear the tumult and are still.' The very air of the place seems to breathe a spirit of philosophical poetry; to stir the thoughts, to touch the heart with pity, as the drowsy forest rustles to the sighing gale.

Hazlitt admired Jaques, calling him 'the only purely contemplative character in Shakespeare'. In productions up to 1842, the famous description of the sobbing deer continued to be given to him rather than to the First Lord as in the Folio text. The picture it presented became a popular subject for painters, including William Blake (1757–1827). His speech on the seven ages was also a popular subject for illustration and often sentimentalised beyond recognition.

In the eighteenth and nineteenth centuries *As You Like It* was not always performed entire. The part of Touchstone was sometimes moderated and any hint of bawdiness elsewhere generally expunged, resulting in a more sentimental version. In the twentieth century, Shakespeare's bawdy has been regarded as an integral part of his vision of things and increased study of Elizabethan English has brought scholars to a greater awareness of its extent.

Edward Tomarken, *As You Like It from 1600 to the Present: Critical Essays*, New York, Garland Publishing, 1997

A substantial book devoted to this play; it includes the text of *Love in a Forest*. The essays, not all by academics, includes accounts of the experiences of directors and actors

Brian Vickers, ed., *William Shakespeare: The Critical Heritage*, 6 vols, Routledge, 1974

This is the fullest compilation of Shakespeare criticism arranged chronologically from the seventeenth century through to the nineteenth. The judgements of earlier writers can be found here. Through use of the indices readers can construct their own account of the evolving critical response to the play. It includes notices of early performances

THE TWENTIETH CENTURY

The tendency of American **New Criticism** of the 1930s and 1940s and in Britain of the school inspired by F.R. Leavis, editor of the influential periodical *Scrutiny* (1932–53), was to treat works of literature as autonomous entities. The essay in *Scrutiny* by James Smith identifies an underlying pattern in which various kinds of melancholy, most prominently in Jaques but present to a lesser degree in other characters, is condemned and dispelled: 'A single *motif* is repeated, giving unity to the whole; but at the same time it varies continually, so that the whole is complex'.

Unlike the history plays, and unlike the realistic satirical city comedies of Ben Jonson, for example, the comedies of Shakespeare with their imaginary worlds do not have any obvious connection with their historical moment that immediately prompts discussion, elucidation and appraisal. Traditional academic criticism that has looked to the background of the play has tended to discuss it and its characters in thematic or generic terms, that is to talk about Shakespeare's relation with his sources and the relation of the play to the literary traditions of both previous comedy and of **romance** and **pastoral**. The essay on the play by Harold Jenkins well exemplifies criticism of this kind.

James Smith, '*As You Like It*', *Scrutiny* 9.1, Cambridge University Press, 1940

Harold Jenkins, '*As You Like It*', *Shakespeare Survey* 8, Cambridge University Press, 1955

HISTORICAL CRITICISM

A seminal essay that has much in common with traditional academic criticism but also seeks to view the play in the light of a complex of Elizabethan ideas about saturnalian customs and holiday-making is that of C.L. Barber. A number of modern studies seek to put the play more firmly in its contemporary social and cultural context and might be regarded as examples of the **New Historicism** in which works of literature are treated not as an autonomous artefacts transcending their time and representing universal truths but as products basically enmeshed in history and in which are encoded larger clashes of social forces and cultural values which they cannot transcend but only reflect. For example, whereas Hazlitt regarded the play as a purely imaginary evocation of an ideal world where the Duke and his followers roam freely in the forest like Robin Hood of old, recent critics, reminding us that Robin Hood was an outlaw who resisted the tyranny of King John, have seen an oblique connection with a contentious contemporary issue: the forcible enclosure of farmland for sheep's grazing. Those who resisted this fled to the forest to live like Robin Hood, as outlaws poaching the sovereign's deer.

A recent evaluation of the play in its historical and social context, which results in an original and stimulating analysis of it, is the account by Louis Adrian Montrose starting, as his title suggests (see below), with the relation between brothers and identifying at the heart of the play's thematic construction a social process that has to do with them. Starting from the undoubted truth that critics like Jenkins have regarded the opening of the play as important only in setting up the circumstances that lead to its essential business, love in a forest, he asks the question, suppose the opposite is true and that love in the forest is the not really the play's raison d'être but merely a means to an end, the end being the remedying of Orlando's situation at the beginning as a victim of primogeniture, the provision in English custom if not law that does not divide inherited property between sons but gives all to the first born? He argues that Rosalind's exuberance has dazzled and bewitched critics and audiences, pointing out, as have others, that while she finally reverts to the position of subordination in which women were held by both law and custom in the sixteenth century, Orlando, however, inherits the earth, emerging triumphant, with property, status and a princess. Orlando's social identity, denied at the beginning when he is the subordinated and socially disadvantaged younger son, is reconstituted by the end, in the process of which he also acquires a surrogate father. The play may be regarded as a wishful fantasy for younger sons and one in which brotherhood is established as an ideal together with a new ideal of nurturing fatherhood in Duke Senior. Despite the fact that it is a woman who steals the show, at the show's end not very much is offered to women (how significant is it that there are no mothers, or even mention of them in the play?); it is the male bond between brothers and the relation between the generations that is repaired and transformed. This transformation is a spiritual renewal as much as a matter of gaining or redistributing property. Montrose provides ample evidence from contemporary documents that the plight of younger sons was a real social phenomenon much noted and talked about at the time.

His analysis also makes sense of a number of slightly puzzling motifs. He argues that the point of the rowdy horn song elicited by Jaques in Act IV Scene 2 is a kind of affirmation of the male principle that all men are joined in potency even if it is that which makes them cuckolds. In another instance the female principle which is undoubtedly an attraction in the play as a whole, might be seen to be a threat as well. Montrose draws attention to a significant change that Shakespeare has made to his source in making the snake and the lion he found there both insidiously female. Rosalind has just teased Orlando about the shrewishness and promiscuity that men can expect from their wives. Montrose argues that the elimination of the insidious threat posed by the snake and the lioness represents symbolically not only the triumph of kindness when brother spares brother but also the mastery of Rosalind's challenge. Her exuberance is finally contained.

Here is the larger view that stresses that comedy, although it may allow a temporary licence to anarchic tendencies, is ultimately conservative since in the end the status quo is restored. At the end of *As You Like It*, Rosalind surrenders her power, yielding to her father and to her husband with identical words to both, 'To you I give myself, for I am yours' (V.4.113).

Harold Bloom, ed., *William Shakespeare's As You Like It*, Modern Critical Interpretations, New York, Chelsea House Publishers, 1988

A selection of critical essays from 1959–86 starting with a chapter from C. L. Barber (cited above), including the chapter of Erickson (cited in the next section) and the article of Montrose

C.L. Barber, 'The Alliance of Seriousness and Levity in *As You Like It*' in *Shakespeare's Festive Comedy: A Study of Dramatic Form and its Relation to Social Custom*, Princeton University Press, 1959

Louis Adrian Montrose, '"The Place of a Brother" in *As You Like It*: Social Process and Comic Form' *Shakespeare Quarterly* 32 no.1, Folgar Shakespeare Library, 1982

Richard Wilson, 'Like the Old Robin Hood: *As You Like It* and the Enclosure Riots' in *Will Power*, Harvester Wheatsheaf, 1993

FEMINIST/GENDER CRITICISM

By far the most influential trend in recent criticism of the play has been prompted by the feminist movement of recent decades and is reflected in the greater interest in, and awareness of, the issues of gender raised by the representation in the play of the masculine and feminine – now increasingly regarded as social and cultural constructions. It may be said that there is lively discussion of the play in relation to the politics of gender.

Although in the conventional ending Rosalind submits to the authority of her husband and her father, many critics would argue that the ending, while it may be said to satisfy convention, cannot altogether eradicate or cancel the effect of Rosalind's assertive behaviour that has come before. Once out, it is difficult to get the genie back into the bottle.

Critics that make a case for the transgressive effect of the comedy point to the general context of disapproval for such theatrical representations. Conservative elements in Elizabethan society, a notable example of which are Puritans who attacked what they regarded as the abuses of the stage, objected generally to the theatre as an institution that encouraged questionable behaviour, and in particular looked askance at the practice of cross-dressing as confusing and disrupting proper social and gender roles as supposedly prescribed by biology and confirmed by

Holy Scripture. Against this disapproving background for the theatre where women were represented on stage by adolescent boys, plays that played around with disguise might be thought to be doubly confusing and suspect, upsetting and disordering the God-given hierarchy in which women were always subordinate to men.

Rosalind, disguised as a boy, commands Orlando to woo her as if she is his Rosalind. In effect, an adolescent boy plays the part of a woman playing the part of a boy playing the part of a woman. All this is wonderfully intriguingly or disturbingly complicated, depending on the spectator's point of view. 'She' is empowered by the disguise and gets away with it, allowing the thought that perhaps gender differences are largely a matter of wearing the right clothes and donning the right behavioural traits to go with them. In playing the part of a woman for Orlando, she refuses to assume the stereotypical role in which he seeks to cast her (the idealised **Petrarchan** beloved) and exposes it for what it is. In the course of her disguise, Rosalind's impatient question when Celia does not immediately tell her the name of suitor 'Dost thou think, though I am caparisoned like a man, I have doublet and hose in my disposition?' (III.2.188–90) calls attention to a stereotypical difference in the behaviour of the sexes. Later on hearing of Orlando's bloody wound, she faints. In these instances it could be said that her own words and behaviour in revealing that she has the weaknesses traditionally associated with women intensify gender difference and make her a non-threatening figure. But questions are raised.

Although these questions may seem to have been laid to rest by the marriages at the end, they are again raised in the epilogue, spoken by Rosalind fully conscious that, 'It is not the fashion for the lady to speak the epilogue' (V.4.196). Her final appeal teasingly draws attention to the fact that she is not a woman, 'If I were a woman, I would kiss as many of you as had beards that pleased me, complexions that liked me, and breaths that I defied not' (V.4.211–13). Shakespeare is teasing his audience by breaking the dramatic illusion to remind his audience of the illusion of disguise inherent in all Elizabethan drama. This is the final tease of many in relation to the disguise in *As You Like It*. It is a reminder that men have been paying court to boys in the course of the play. In this connection the name of the Greek name Ganymede (also in Thomas Lodge), the beautiful Trojan youth stolen by the king of the gods to be his cupbearer, is thought-provoking, and the thoughts that it provokes have to do with the usually forbidden subject of same sex attraction. The teasing plot of *As You Like It* touches lightly upon so many of the issues of sexual identity that have become such a conscious and serious preoccupation in modern criticism and indeed modern living.

Barbara J. Bono, 'Mixed Gender, Mixed Genre in Shakespeare's *As You Like It*', in *Renaissance Genres: Essays on Theory, History and Interpretation*, edited by Barbara K. Lewlaski, Harvard University Press, 1986

Juliet Dusinberre, 'As *Who* Liked It', *Shakespeare Survey* 46, Cambridge University Press, 1994

Peter Erickson, 'Sexual Politics and Social Structure in *As You Like It*' in *Patriarchal Structures in Shakespeare's Drama*, University of California, 1985

Jean Howard, 'Power and Eros: Crossdressing in Dramatic Representation and Theatrical Practice' in *The Stage and Social Struggle in Early Modern England*, Routledge, 1994

Valerie Traub, 'The Homoerotics of Shakespeare's Comedy' in *Desire and Anxiety: Circulations of Sexuality in Shakespearean Drama*, Routledge, 1992

OTHER STUDIES

Systematic academic study has sought to put Shakespeare in his literary context and to relate the play to the tradition of comedy and to his source material.

T.W. Baldwin, *William Shakspere's Smalle Latine and Lesse Greeke*, 2 vols, University of Illinois Press, 1944

> This voluminous work of scholarship based upon a close examination of the learning that can be gleaned from his plays attempts to recreate what Shakespeare gained from the classical education he is likely to have had at Stratford grammar school. The character of Touchstone, for example, is related to the teaching of rhetoric and logic in the schools

Geoffrey Bullough, ed., *Narrative and Dramatic Sources of Shakespeare*, vol. 2, Macmillan, 1964

This is the standard work, containing the main sources, chiefly Lodge's *Rosalynde*

Leo Salingar, *Shakespeare and the Traditions of Comedy*, Cambridge University Press, 1974

As the title suggests, this sets Shakespeare's comedy against his ancient and Italian Renaissance antecedents and his immediate English predecessors

Stanley Wells, *The Cambridge Companion to Shakespeare*, Cambridge University Press, 1991

A handy volume containing general information and background for beginners

World events	Shakespeare's life	Literary events
		1516 Thomas More, *Utopia*
		1532 Machiavelli, *The Prince*
	1557 John Shakespeare marries Mary Arden	
1558 The French capture Calais		
	1564 William Shakespeare is born	
1565 Sir John Hawkins brings tobacco to England		
1576 First theatre in England opens at Shoreditch		
		1578 John Lyly, *Euphues: The Anatomy of Wit*
1581 Conversion to Roman Catholicism is deemed treason in England		
1582 Plague breaks out in London	**1582** Shakespeare marries Anne Hathaway	
1583 Newfoundland is claimed for Elizabeth I by Gilbert	**1583** A daughter, Susanna, is born	
	1585 The twins, Hamnet and Judith, are born	
1588 Spanish Armada defeated		
	late 1580s - early 1590s Shakespeare probably writes *Henry VI*, parts I, II & III and *Richard III*	
		1590 Thomas Lodge, *Rosalynde;* Sir Philip Sidney, *The Countess of Pembroke's Arcadia*
	1592 Shakespeare acting in London	
	1592-4 He writes *The Comedy of Errors*	
1593-1606 Ottoman expansion into Europe halted by prolonged war with Austria		
	1594 Shakespeare writes exclusively for the Lord Chamberlain's Men	**1594-5** Vincentio Saviolo, *His Practise of the Rapier and Dagger*
1595-1603 Tyrone's rebellion in Ireland	**1595** *Two Gentlemen of Verona, The Taming of the Shrew* and *Love's Labours Lost* are thought to have been completed by this time. He writes *Romeo and Juliet*	

World events	Shakespeare's life	Literary events
1596 Francis Drake perishes on an expedition to the West Indies	**1596-8** *Henry IV*, parts 1 & 2 written	
1598 First mention of the game of cricket	**1598-9** Globe Theatre built at Southwark	
	1598-1600 ***As You Like It***	
	1599 *Henry V* completed	
	1600 *A Midsummer Night's Dream*, *Much Ado about Nothing* and *The Merchant of Venice* printed. *Twelfth Night* and *Julius Caesar* probably written	
	1600-1 *Hamlet* written	
	1602 *Troilus and Cressida* probably written	
1603 Elizabeth I dies	**1603** His company becomes the King's Men, patronised by James I, the new king	
	1604 *Othello* performed	**1604** James I, *A Counterblast to Tobacco*
1605 Discovery of Guy Fawkes' plot to destroy Parliament	**1605** First version of *King Lear*	**1605** Cervantes, *Don Quixote*
	1606 Shakespeare writes *Macbeth*	**1606** Ben Johnson, *Volpone*
	1606-7 *Antony and Cleopatra* probably written	
1607 English Parliament rejects union between England and Scotland		
	1608 The King's Men acquire Blackfriar's Theatre for winter performances	
1610 Use of the fork for eating spreads from Italy to England	**1610** *Coriolanus* written	
	1611 Shakespeare retires to his house in Stratford	
1612 Last burning of heretics in England		**1612** John Webster, *The White Devil*
	1613 Globe Theatre burns down	
	1616 Shakespeare dies	
1620 The Mayflower takes the Pilgrim Fathers to Massachusetts		

alliteration a sequence of repeated consonantal sounds in a stretch of language. The matching consonants are usually at the beginning of words or stressed syllables. It is common in poetry and prose, and is one of the most easily identifiable figures of speech

antithesis (from the Greek meaning 'opposite placing') a rhetorical term describing the opposition of contrasting ideas in neighbouring sentences or clauses, using opposite or contrasting forms of words. For examples, see the section on language in Critical Approaches

assonance the use of the same vowel sounds with different consonants in successive words or stressed syllables e.g. nation and traitor

denouement (Fr. 'unknotting') the final unfolding of a plot: the point at which the reader's expectations, be they hopes or fears, about what will happen to the characters are finally satisfied or denied. The denouement of *As You Like It* occurs when Rosalind dispenses with her disguise

dramatic irony a feature of many plays: it occurs when the development of the plot allows the audience to possess more information about what is happening than some of the characters themselves have. In *As You like It* only Touchstone knows that Rosalind and Celia are in disguise in the Forest of Arden. Characters may also speak in a dramatically ironic way, saying something that points to events to come without understanding the significance of what they say

euphuism derived from the title of the courtier John Lyly's prose romance *Euphues: The Anatomy of Wit* (1578) and describing the style he made fashionable and famous there. This witty, elegant and learned style is marked by concentrated use of antithesis and balance in its vocabulary and sentence structure together with a marked use of alliteration to the extent that it became highly mannered. An example is quoted and discussed in Literary Background. Its influence can be felt in Shakespeare's prose. The adjective euphues in Greek means 'well natured'

genre a distinct kind of literature, such as pastoral, epic, romance or detective fiction with its own conventions and characteristics. These are never fixed; if they were, change and development would be impossible, but knowledge of the conventions and characteristics made famous in archetypes of the kind which writers may work with or may manipulate and vary can often help in the understanding and appreciation of works of literature. *As You Like It* is usually considered to be generically mixed; a comic mixture of elements from romance and pastoral

Intentional fallacy American New Critics introduced this term for what they regarded as the mistaken critical method of judging a literary work according to the author's intentions, whether stated or implied. They argued that the value and meaning of each literary work resides solely in the text itself

malcontent the malcontent came to be a stock character in Elizabethan and Jacobean literature, the alienated and disgruntled outsider who laments the state of the world. Jaques bears some resemblance to the type

masque a courtly entertainment popular in the Renaissance, in which masqued actors offered a performance of dignified spectacle. Rosalind introduces Hymen, the god of marriage, as a masquer. This is a formal device to lend dignity and solemnity to the proceedings

metaphor a figure of speech in which a word or phrase is applied to an object or action that it does not literally denote in order to imply a resemblance

New Criticism a major critical movement that recommended that a poem must be studied as a poem and not as a piece of biographical or sociological evidence, or literary-historical material, or as a demonstration of a psychological theory of literature, or for any other reason. Close reading of texts became the only legitimate critical procedure seeing the work as a linguistic structure

New Historicism the work of critics who discuss literary works in terms of their historical contexts, often minutely researched, as a reaction against New Criticism and Structuralism

pastoral from the Latin *pastor* meaning shepherd. A mannered, artificial and non-realistic form of literature in which the characters are presented in the guise of shepherds living a simple life in the country away from civilisation, whether in the city or at court. In classical pastoral, the idyllic landscape of Arcadia came to be the beautiful backdrop of life in the Golden Age, a mythical time of peace, innocence and justice when man lived in an eternal springtime and in harmony with nature who supplied all his needs spontaneously without the help of the plough. With the advent of agriculture followed by commerce and civilisation, human greed and aggression have taken over; the Golden Age has receded and left mankind in our present Age of Iron. Pastoral is a nostalgic mode looking back to a never-never-land of simple innocence and represents a desire to escape from the strains and stresses of advanced civilisation into a simpler world of the imagination. The shepherds of pastoral traditionally have enough time on their hands to sing beautifully of their love affairs which are conducted in a courtly and romantic fashion; pastorals are often populated by love-sick swains lamenting their unrequited love in stylised language and feeling rather sorry for themselves. Silvius is an archetype of literary pastoral, cruelly faced with an unrequited love. The aged Corin, on the other hand, is a more realistic shepherd who has to worry about the selling of his lands. The Forest of Arden is not described like the classical Arcadia; it is more realistic, in fact it is a harsh place whose inhabitants have to suffer the hardships of winter. Yet the life lived in it is presented idealistically in contrast to life at 'the envious court' (II.1.4).

pastoral romance a generic mix combining elements of both pastoral (see above) and romance (see below). Thomas Lodge's *Rosalynde* (1590) (described in Critical Approaches) the main source of *As You Like It* is an example of a this form which was popular in Elizabethan England. The most famous example is Sir Philip Sidney's *The Countesse of Pembroke's Arcadia* (1590)

Petrarchanism Imitating the style and subject matter of the Italian poet Petrarch (1304–74). Though he wrote various kinds of poetry, it is his *Canzoinere* (c.1335), sonnets in the Provencal courtly love tradition, which was so influential in shaping lyric poetry, especially during the sixteenth century. The poems are dedicated to the idealised memory of a woman called Laura; they are filled with highly rhetorical expressions of his passion, including conceits, far-fetched comparisons, concerning the effects of love on his changing mood. The idealising mode that is mocked in the play owes something to this still popular tradition

romance (in medieval Latin 'in the romance language') Primarily medieval fictions in verse or prose dealing with adventures of chivalry and love. 'Romance' originally meant a work written in the French language. The form developed in twelfth-century France and spread to other countries. Verse gave way to prose as the popular medium. Romance characteristically describes a sophisticated courtly world of chivalry, distinct from the heroic epic, which concentrated on war. Typical stories concern knightly quests, tournaments, magic, and contests with monsters for the sake of a heroine who is the focus for courtly love, but many of the tales have a strong moral content. The wrestling match, the testing (though not the teasing) of the hero, the stark antithesis between good and evil, the incident with the snake and the lioness, Rosalind's uncle versed in magic (though he is fictional, he comes from the world of romance and his reality is not questioned by the Duke or Orlando) all could be said to be romantic ingredients

soliloquy (from the Latin 'to speak alone') dramatic convention which allows a character in a play to speak directly to the audience as if thinking aloud about motives, feelings and decisions

structuralism and post-structuralism structuralism examines aspects of human society, including language, literature and social institutions, as integrated structures or systems in which the parts have no real existence of their own, but derive meaning and significance only from their place within the system. For example, the basic unit of meaning in language, the phoneme (basic sound unit), is seen to derive its meaning not from any inherent qualities in itself, but because of its 'difference' from other sounds. Structuralist critics often explore individual works in literature by analysing them in terms of linguistic concepts, like the phoneme, or as if the structure of a work resembled the syntax of a sentence. Others concentrate on examining the conventions and expectations which a knowledgeable reader understands implicitly when reading the work, with the ultimate aim of building up a kind of grammar or ground-plan of the whole system of literature and its place in society.

Structuralism has now been superseded by the even more radical post-structuralist theories, also known as deconstruction

syntax the arrangement of words in their appropriate forms and proper order, in order to achieve meaning

tragicomedy a mixture of tragedy and comedy

wit (from old English 'to know') originally meaning 'sense', 'understanding' or 'intelligence' as used by Shakespeare and as used about him, it refers to that sharp verbal intelligence and ingenuity embodied to excess in Touchstone and exemplified more genially though often sharply in Rosalind.

wordplay playing on and with words, often for humorous effect by the use of puns, where the play is between two words of identical sounds but different meanings. There are many bawdy *double entendres* ('double hearings') particularly in Touchstone's language. Touchstone is master of another kind of extended wordplay, *quibbling* 'arguing in a purely verbal way' that is, evading the issue by deliberately playing with words, often by taking them too literally. Wordplay is a persistent feature of this play and not always for humorous effect (see the section on language in Critical Approaches)

Author of this note

Robin Sowerby studied Classics and English at Cambridge. He now lectures in the Department of English Studies at Stirling University. He has written York Notes on Homer's *Iliad* and *Odyssey*, Virgil's *Aeneid*, Plato's *Republic* and an advanced note on Shakespeare's *Antony and Cleopatra*. He has edited selections from Dryden and Pope and is the author of *The Classical Legacy in Renaissance Poetry*, Longman, 1994.

NOTES

Notes

NOTES

NOTES

NOTES

NOTES

NOTES

Notes

York Notes Advanced (£3.99 each)

Margaret Atwood
The Handmaid's Tale

Jane Austen
Mansfield Park

Jane Austen
Persuasion

Jane Austen
Pride and Prejudice

Alan Bennett
Talking Heads

William Blake
Songs of Innocence and of Experience

Charlotte Brontë
Jane Eyre

Emily Brontë
Wuthering Heights

Geoffrey Chaucer
The Franklin's Tale

Geoffrey Chaucer
General Prologue to the Canterbury Tales

Geoffrey Chaucer
The Wife of Bath's Prologue and Tale

Joseph Conrad
Heart of Darkness

Charles Dickens
Great Expectations

John Donne
Selected Poems

George Eliot
The Mill on the Floss

F. Scott Fitzgerald
The Great Gatsby

E.M. Forster
A Passage to India

Brian Friel
Translations

Thomas Hardy
The Mayor of Casterbridge

Thomas Hardy
Tess of the d'Urbervilles

Seamus Heaney
Selected Poems from Opened Ground

Nathaniel Hawthorne
The Scarlet Letter

James Joyce
Dubliners

John Keats
Selected Poems

Christopher Marlowe
Doctor Faustus

Arthur Miller
Death of a Salesman

Toni Morrison
Beloved

William Shakespeare
Antony and Cleopatra

William Shakespeare
As You Like It

William Shakespeare
Hamlet

William Shakespeare
King Lear

William Shakespeare
Measure for Measure

William Shakespeare
The Merchant of Venice

William Shakespeare
Much Ado About Nothing

William Shakespeare
Othello

William Shakespeare
Romeo and Juliet

William Shakespeare
The Tempest

William Shakespeare
The Winter's Tale

Mary Shelley
Frankenstein

Alice Walker
The Color Purple

Oscar Wilde
The Importance of Being Earnest

Tennessee Williams
A Streetcar Named Desire

John Webster
The Duchess of Malfi

W.B. Yeats
Selected Poems

GCSE and equivalent levels (£3.50 each)

Maya Angelou
I Know Why the Caged Bird Sings

Jane Austen
Pride and Prejudice

Alan Ayckbourn
Absent Friends

Elizabeth Barrett Browning
Selected Poems

Robert Bolt
A Man for All Seasons

Harold Brighouse
Hobson's Choice

Charlotte Brontë
Jane Eyre

Emily Brontë
Wuthering Heights

Shelagh Delaney
A Taste of Honey

Charles Dickens
David Copperfield

Charles Dickens
Great Expectations

Charles Dickens
Hard Times

Charles Dickens
Oliver Twist

Roddy Doyle
Paddy Clarke Ha Ha Ha

George Eliot
Silas Marner

George Eliot
The Mill on the Floss

William Golding
Lord of the Flies

Oliver Goldsmith
She Stoops To Conquer

Willis Hall
The Long and the Short and the Tall

Thomas Hardy
Far from the Madding Crowd

Thomas Hardy
The Mayor of Casterbridge

Thomas Hardy
Tess of the d'Urbervilles

Thomas Hardy
The Withered Arm and other Wessex Tales

L.P. Hartley
The Go-Between

Seamus Heaney
Selected Poems

Susan Hill
I'm the King of the Castle

Barry Hines
A Kestrel for a Knave

Louise Lawrence
Children of the Dust

Harper Lee
To Kill a Mockingbird

Laurie Lee
Cider with Rosie

Arthur Miller
The Crucible

Arthur Miller
A View from the Bridge

Robert O'Brien
Z for Zachariah

Frank O'Connor
My Oedipus Complex and other stories

George Orwell
Animal Farm

J.B. Priestley
An Inspector Calls

Willy Russell
Educating Rita

Willy Russell
Our Day Out

J.D. Salinger
The Catcher in the Rye

William Shakespeare
Henry IV Part 1

William Shakespeare
Henry V

William Shakespeare
Julius Caesar

William Shakespeare
Macbeth

William Shakespeare
The Merchant of Venice

William Shakespeare
A Midsummer Night's Dream

William Shakespeare
Much Ado About Nothing

William Shakespeare
Romeo and Juliet

William Shakespeare
The Tempest

William Shakespeare
Twelfth Night

George Bernard Shaw
Pygmalion

Mary Shelley
Frankenstein

R.C. Sherriff
Journey's End

Rukshana Smith
Salt on the snow

John Steinbeck
Of Mice and Men

Robert Louis Stevenson
Dr Jekyll and Mr Hyde

Jonathan Swift
Gulliver's Travels

Robert Swindells
Daz 4 Zoe

Mildred D. Taylor
Roll of Thunder, Hear My Cry

Mark Twain
Huckleberry Finn

James Watson
Talking in Whispers

William Wordsworth
Selected Poems

A Choice of Poets

Mystery Stories of the Nineteenth Century including The Signalman

Nineteenth Century Short Stories

Poetry of the First World War

Six Women Poets

FUTURE TITLES IN THE YORK NOTES SERIES

Chinua Achebe
Things Fall Apart

Edward Albee
Who's Afraid of Virginia Woolf?

Margaret Atwood
Cat's Eye

Jane Austen
Emma

Jane Austen
Northanger Abbey

Jane Austen
Sense and Sensibility

Samuel Beckett
Waiting for Godot

Robert Browning
Selected Poems

Robert Burns
Selected Poems

Angela Carter
Nights at the Circus

Geoffrey Chaucer
The Merchant's Tale

Geoffrey Chaucer
The Miller's Tale

Geoffrey Chaucer
The Nun's Priest's Tale

Samuel Taylor Coleridge
Selected Poems

Daniel Defoe
Moll Flanders

Daniel Defoe
Robinson Crusoe

Charles Dickens
Bleak House

Charles Dickens
Hard Times

Emily Dickinson
Selected Poems

Carol Ann Duffy
Selected Poems

George Eliot
Middlemarch

T.S. Eliot
The Waste Land

T.S. Eliot
Selected Poems

Henry Fielding
Joseph Andrews

E.M. Forster
Howards End

John Fowles
The French Lieutenant's Woman

Robert Frost
Selected Poems

Elizabeth Gaskell
North and South

Stella Gibbons
Cold Comfort Farm

Graham Greene
Brighton Rock

Thomas Hardy
Jude the Obscure

Thomas Hardy
Selected Poems

Joseph Heller
Catch-22

Homer
The Iliad

Homer
The Odyssey

Gerard Manley Hopkins
Selected Poems

Aldous Huxley
Brave New World

Kazuo Ishiguro
The Remains of the Day

Ben Jonson
The Alchemist

Ben Jonson
Volpone

James Joyce
A Portrait of the Artist as a Young Man

Philip Larkin
Selected Poems

D.H. Lawrence
The Rainbow

D.H. Lawrence
Selected Stories

D.H. Lawrence
Sons and Lovers

D.H. Lawrence
Women in Love

John Milton
Paradise Lost Bks I & II

John Milton
Paradise Lost Bks IV & IX

Thomas More
Utopia

Sean O'Casey
Juno and the Paycock

George Orwell
Nineteen Eighty-four

John Osborne
Look Back in Anger

Wilfred Owen
Selected Poems

Sylvia Plath
Selected Poems

Alexander Pope
Rape of the Lock and other poems

Ruth Prawer Jhabvala
Heat and Dust

Jean Rhys
Wide Sargasso Sea

William Shakespeare
As You Like It

William Shakespeare
Coriolanus

William Shakespeare
Henry IV Pt 1

William Shakespeare
Henry V

William Shakespeare
Julius Caesar

William Shakespeare
Macbeth

William Shakespeare
Measure for Measure

William Shakespeare
A Midsummer Night's Dream

William Shakespeare
Richard II

William Shakespeare
Richard III

William Shakespeare
Sonnets

William Shakespeare
The Taming of the Shrew

William Shakespeare
Twelfth Night

William Shakespeare
The Winter's Tale

George Bernard Shaw
Arms and the Man

George Bernard Shaw
Saint Joan

Muriel Spark
The Prime of Miss Jean Brodie

John Steinbeck
The Grapes of Wrath

John Steinbeck
The Pearl

Tom Stoppard
Arcadia

Tom Stoppard
Rosencrantz and Guildenstern are Dead

Jonathan Swift
Gulliver's Travels and The Modest Proposal

Alfred, Lord Tennyson
Selected Poems

W.M. Thackeray
Vanity Fair

Virgil
The Aeneid

Edith Wharton
The Age of Innocence

Tennessee Williams
Cat on a Hot Tin Roof

Tennessee Williams
The Glass Menagerie

Virginia Woolf
Mrs Dalloway

Virginia Woolf
To the Lighthouse

William Wordsworth
Selected Poems

Metaphysical Poets